Dayenu — Freedom Enough

Out of inner slavery into perfect fulfilment

Bibliografische Information der Deutschen Nationalbibliothek:
Die Deutsche Nationalbibliothek verzeichnet diese Publikation in der Deutschen Nationalbibliografie; detaillierte bibliografische Daten sind im Internet über http://dnb.dnb.de abrufbar.

© 2022 Dorothea Lehmann

Cover: Danielle Dempwolf

Revision: Tobias Liebig, Susan Castell, Henning Rietz, Kerstin Zedler and Stefanie Stanislawiak

Contact: dajenu.buch@gmx.de

Production and publishing: BoD - Books on Demand, Norderstedt

ISBN: 978-3-7392-1941-7

Dedication

In loving memory of my father, whose love for the God of Israel and no less for me laid the foundation of my life.

Inhalt

Dedication 7

Dayenu introduced – a prologue 11

Dayenu revealed 13

   That's what a revelation feels like 15

Dayenu told 18

   What is freedom? 18

   Why God makes such an effort 21

   How does God do it? 24

   The 15 steps into perfect freedom 26

Deliverance Enough 29

   The Five Stanzas of Leaving Slavery 29

   If He had brought us out of Egypt 32

   If he had carried out judgement against them 39

   If he had destroyed their idols 47

   If he had slain the firstborn 54

   If he had given us their wealth 60

   God's perfect deliverance 64

Provision Enough 66

    The Five Stanzas of Miracles 66

    If he had split the sea for us 69

    If he had taken us through the sea on dry land 77

    If he had drowned our oppressors in the sea 81

    If he had supplied for our needs in the desert for 40 years 87

    If he had fed us manna 98

    God's perfect provision 104

Fulfilment enough 107

    The Five Stanzas of Closeness with God 107

    If he had given us the Shabbat 109

    If he had brought us before Mount Sinai 119

    If he had given us the Torah 130

    If he had brought us into the land of Israel 140

    If he had built the Holy Temple for us 149

    God's perfect fulfilment 158

Dayenu fulfilled 161

Truly enough 161

Perfect fulfilment through perfect peace 166

So where am I? 169

As for me and my household 173

Dayenu applied – an epilogue 176

Dayenu introduced – a prologue

This book is about freedom. Not just any freedom, but perfect heavenly freedom. The freedom to truly be who we are and to know God as he truly is. I never set out to write about that subject. I never even thought much about it before the Holy Spirit basically let it fall into my lap. With one comparatively small revelation while sitting at my parents' dinner table he showed me one of God's general principles: His process of liberation exemplified in the story of the Exodus. The Spirit showed me the steps God takes to deliver from slavery into perfect freedom, perfect provision, and perfect fulfilment. He showed me that the same steps he took Israel out of Egypt into the Promised Land are the steps he takes us out of our sin into a deep relationship with him. He showed me how God is the same yesterday, today, and tomorrow. So he still works the same way, reveals himself the same way, delivers me the same way as he did his people. And how the principles he established with a whole nation apply just as much on a smaller scale, when it is just me he wants to set free.

Since the initial revelation as well as my subsequent dive into the meaning of it was a very intimate walk with and towards God, I decided for this book to also focus more on what this means for an individual person and their path to God's heart. But I know from experience that if I start with my own life, align myself with God, let him lead me into freedom, and strive to know him as he is, it will soon seep into my relationships, my family, my community, and the world. And the more I internalize God's process of freedom with me as an individual, the easier it is to observe how those same principles still apply in more general settings and on bigger scales: in families, communities, nations, and even history.

I found, no matter whether he guides the world to freedom and unto himself, or a community, a family, or just little old me, God always takes the same route. It is a route worth studying and a journey well worth taking because the ultimate destination is where we were made to be: A deep fulfilling relationship with the God who loves us.

Dayenu revealed

Everything written in this book started with my Dad. He probably wouldn't see it that way, because he never thought much of himself, but it is true. And since he is not with us anymore, he cannot object to the attention this might bring. It all started with him because his life, far more than his words, spoke about God's unfailing, unchanging goodness. For his christening, his confirmation, and his funeral he had the same bible verse. What had been a coincidence at his confirmation, he insisted upon for his funeral:

> *The precepts of the Lord are right, giving joy to the heart.*
> *(Psalm 19:8)[1]*

Planning for his impending passing my Mom had suggested, he might want to pick a new verse, but Dad would have none of it. To him it was a clear word from God, a blessing, and a credo, that wouldn't change, just like God had never changed throughout his life. He lived by these words, experienced the joy given by following God's precepts, and always sought a deeper understanding of God's perfect goodness. One step he undertook to encounter God on a deeper level was travelling to the land of the Bible. The first time in his twenties and on several occasions in later years. There he experienced something special, something Jesus himself had been alluding to in Luke 19:40. The stones cried out, giving testimony of God's unfailing, unchanging faithfulness towards his people. I, too, have had this experience, this revelation that

---

[1] If not stated otherwise, all Bible quotes are taken from the New International Version of 2011.

God is still holding up his covenant with Israel to this day. I, too, have had this glimpse into God's unchanging love for the Israelites and, by extension, for us as the grafted olive branch. And I fell in love with the God of Abraham, Isaac, and Israel all over again, just like my father had done over thirty years before me.

To my Dad, loving the God of Israel meant learning Hebrew, so he could read the Bible and talk to his Heavenly Father in his chosen language. It meant learning and following God's commandments, and it meant living and commemorating the rituals and holidays God had decreed his people to celebrate. So, my Dad's love for God, his people, and his commandments meant that I basically grew up in a semi-Jewish household. And the only reason it had to be called semi was that our Jewish roots are too far back to be proven nowadays. Had my father been more of an enforcer rather than the mild-mannered unassuming man he was, we probably would have dropped the semi long ago.

I am eternally grateful for my father's devotion to the God of Israel. First and foremost because it taught me a desire to know God and make him known as the person he truly is. To seek his goodness even in the difficult, demanding parts of his word. And to trust him even if I don't understand his actions. This laid the foundation of my faith and to this day forms the building blocks of my relationship with God. I know, in my heart of hearts, I can trust God's goodness in everything. And if I don't see it straight away, I can freely ask the Holy Spirit to reveal his unfailing love behind all of his actions. He will always and gladly answer my plea.

That's what a revelation feels like

When I was growing up my Dad had a printing shop. Huge machines, almost historical looking printing presses, and mountains of paper. I still remember the smell of dry papery air and fresh printing paint. For us kids it was the most exciting albeit slightly dangerous indoor playground we could imagine.

My favourite part was the big cutting machine. It took up half the room, made Star Trek sounds when working and was not at all comparable to the little paper cutters you get in offices. It was strictly off limits for us, which, of course, made it irresistible. My Dad would cut off the tiniest strip from the edge of a 500 sheets stack of paper with perfect precision. And since the resulting waste looked like less sparkly tinsel, I would take it and pretend it was my horse's tail or my beautiful Rapunzel hair or whatever I wanted it to be that day.

I loved watching my Dad work the cutting machine. One part of it stuck with me in particular over the years. It was whenever Dad would cut a large stack of paper in half. Because every time that terribly sharp, futuristic looking blade would glide through the paper with little to no resistance, it seemed as if the knife hadn't really cut the stack but opened an already existing cut. Almost like a book opening up in the middle.

It is that image that pops up in my head when I have one of those moments where the Holy Spirit just reveals the meaning of certain parts of scripture. It's like he comes down with a sword, cutting through a whole stack of paper, opening up a whole book of truth in my mind and I feel like: "Of course! How didn't I see that before? This is brilliant!"

The most mind-blowing experience of that kind I had one evening while I was visiting my parents. It was the evening of Passover Seder, the first night of the Jewish holiday of Passover. My father, driven by his heart for God's people, had over the years accumulated knowledge and expertise in Jewish traditions. So, this particular Seder evening my parents had some Christian friends over to celebrate Jewish Passover while also explaining everything to the "goyim"[2].

I was just there to help my mom in the kitchen and didn't expect to learn anything new since this wasn't my first Seder. My first had been on my tenth birthday and anyone who knows what weird types of food are traditionally served that night can probably understand why I wasn't very enthusiastic about it back then.

So this time I just sat at the table, being a good daughter, going through the motions, leaning, raising the glass, dipping stuff into other stuff, and so on and so forth. Until the Holy Spirit brought down his sword on my head and opened this book of truth in my mind

My Dad had just begun to read the Dayenu, a poem quoting every step of Israel's journey out of slavery into the Promised Land. It's a very compressed telling of stories normally stretching over the books of Exodus, Joshua, Samuel, and Kings. It consists of 15 verses and after every line the father reads, the family answers with

---

[2] Goyim = plural of goy, Yiddish for non-Jew

"Dayenu", which means "That would have sufficed" or "That would have been enough", thus expressing that even just one of these steps would have been enough to praise God forever.

The Holy Spirit brought down his sword simply by saying: "Can you see how that is still the way I save you? These 15 steps out of slavery and into the Promised Land are still the way I lead you out of sin and into my perfect freedom, back into my loving arms."

With every verse of the poem he drove this truth in deeper and deeper. So, this was a pretty deep cut, a pretty thick book of truth opening in my mind. Way more than 500 pages in this stack, to be sure.

Since that night I have been studying this particular book of truth, talked to people about it, and gathered from their reactions how useful this truth can be. It can be a guide through the process of freedom. It can be used as a timeline showing you where you stand right now, revealing the steps already taken and pointing towards upcoming stages. It shows you how God works for your freedom. How he spares nothing to break you free from sin, restriction, and condemnation. It reveals God's heart to you and just might let you understand his actions a bit better. And I sincerely hope it will give you the courage to trust and follow God out of slavery and into your Promised Land.

So here it is: For all to read, hopefully to receive, and maybe to pass along: the truth of Freedom Enough.

Dayenu told

What is freedom?

It is difficult to write about freedom, simply because the word means so many different things to each of us. The meaning of freedom and our understanding of it usually relates to whatever is holding us captive at the moment, to whatever impairs us most, because that is what we want to be free from.

Freedom is very important to us. We lay down the right to freedom in our countries' constitutions and as foundation of our state structures, and are prepared to fight whenever our personal freedom is in danger. Freedom of press, freedom of opinion, freedom of religion, and any other "freedom of", they are all based upon the freedom of choice.

As I am writing this, the Covid-19 pandemic forces the whole world to give up a lot of freedom. When governments decide whether or not people are allowed to travel, go to work, meet with friends, and send their kids to school, the cries for freedom get louder. No matter how much this containment might be in the best interest of the nation. We feel oppressed because we cannot do as we would like. We cannot decide for ourselves.

That is what we really mean by freedom: Self-determination, self-government, self-expression, self-realization, self-fulfilment. The right to choose our own fate and for nobody else to be allowed to interfere. So that we may do with our lives whatever we want.

Even in our churches we mostly live by this worldly definition of freedom. We expect neighbourly Christian love, acceptance without respect of person, grace without judgment, support without correction, mercy without repentance. Because we are set free, aren't we? How dare those brothers and sisters in Christ try and burden us again? At the most they are allowed to give counsel, but it remains our choice to do with it as we see fit.

God, on the other hand, paints a completely different picture of freedom. He made Man as a free being, created him in his own image, as a friend, an equal. Adam and Eve, living in the Garden of Eden, are completely free. Free from pain, free from sickness, free from suffering, free from persecution, free from oppression, free from danger, free from need, free from shame, free from burden, free from sin, free from death. There is nothing holding them in the slightest. Just God.

The only restriction Adam and Eve have to live by is to not eat from the Tree of the Knowledge of Good and Evil, because they would die if they did. This is how the Serpent finds them and, with just one question and one very selective view of the consequences of disobedience, casts the shadow of doubt on God's goodness.

"Did God really say, 'You must not eat from any tree in the garden'?" it asks. "No, we may eat any fruit, just not from the tree that is in the middle of the garden. We would die if we did," Eve answers. "You will not die," replies the Serpent, "God just knows that when you eat from it your eyes will be opened, and you will be like God, knowing Good and Evil." (see Genesis 3:1-5)

Conveniently leaving out that eating the fruit means being separated from God, the giver of all life, the Serpent depicts eating from the Tree of Knowledge as desirable. Insinuating God would have ulterior motives for his restriction. It implies that Adam and Eve could be more than they are now and that God apparently wants to keep that from happening. This changes something in Eve's heart. Enticed by the beauty of the fruit, ensnared by the promise of godlike wisdom, and feeling betrayed by God, she eats the fruit and gives Adam, who is with her, some of it as well.

One little exaggeration, one little distortion of the facts was all it took for Adam and Eve to stop trusting God. And so, like humankind ever since, they didn't feel free anymore unless they could be their own masters. They desired to be free from God. So they ate the fruit and as a result they became enslaved. Became slaves to work, slaves to money, slaves to self-fulfilment, slaves to lust, slaves to addiction, slaves to death.

The independence from God changed everything. Now we suffer pain, sickness, persecution, oppression, danger, need, shame, burden, sin, and all the accompanying worries and consequences. And our "freedom" to do with our lives as we please can't free us from any of it. And the worst part is: we are slaves to being separated from God.

That is something God cannot stand: For us to be doomed to be separated from him and live in slavery and brokenness. He never desired us to be far from him, never wanted us to be crippled by our sin. No, he is committed to bringing us back into his true and lasting freedom, and gives everything to make a way for us to come back to him and to the relationship we were made for. Where we are free from everything and being held only by him.

This is what God means when he talks about freeing us. He means to bring us back to the state of freedom Adam and Eve had in Eden. To be free from sin, sickness, pain, destitution, and death and instead to live in perfect security, unfailing provision, and everlasting fulfilment. That is the freedom we lost with the fall of Man. That is the freedom we traded for independence and self-determination when we ate from the Tree of Knowledge. And that is the freedom God takes great pains to make available to us once more.

Why God makes such an effort

Man eating the fruit must have broken God's heart. His perfect creation, the equals he made to share in the beauty of the world with him so far only knew him as the loving provider of everything they could ever wish for. Now they desire to be their own masters. He knows what us following this desire means for the world, for ourselves, and for our relationship with him: utter destruction and despair. Yet, he respects this decision. It doesn't even surprise him. After all, he planted the Tree of Knowledge himself. He created it precisely to give us the ability to choose whether to stay in our loving but dependent relationship with him or not. He knew what this choice would throw us into and what it would cost him to bring us back, but he provided it anyway. The question is why.

I asked God this once. He must have known that Man would fall. He must have known that we would become slaves to sin and death. He must have known we would need his intervention, his deliverance, mercy, and grace, if we should ever be able to live in his perfect freedom again. He must have known that it would cost him his only begotten son to restore what the Fall of Man destroyed. So I wanted to understand why he would put himself through such devastating pain, if he could have just not planted that treacherous tree in the first place.

The Holy Spirit answered, as he usually does, by bringing down his sword of truth on my mind: "Because I love you. And I wanted you to be free to choose to love me."

He wanted us to be as equal as possible in this relationship. But for us to be equal to the almighty God, he needed to limit his power by putting our will above his own. By deciding that he will respect our decisions, even if he would love to spare us the consequences. So we can have a choice, because love is never forced. This is how much he loves us. He is denying himself, restricting his own sovereignty, and willingly facing the terrible consequence of sacrificing his own son, just to give us the chance to come back to him. Jesus dying on the cross was not Plan B, was not the solution God came up with after Adam and Eve had shocked him with their disobedience. He already knew he would have to make this sacrifice, when he planted the tree. I am convinced God went all in right at the beginning of his story with us. That he was prepared to go all the way, to give up everything to ensure us a way out of the slavery of independence back into his perfect freedom. And I believe his mind was made up, before he even started to create the world, that he would give it his all. To love us without restraint and to fight for us literally to his last breath. He counted up the cost and decided: having us as free equals was worth it.

That is the love Adam and Eve dwelled in in the Garden of Eden. They lived in God's hand, knowing nothing but perfect security, unfailing provision, and everlasting fulfilment. By eating from the Tree of Knowledge Man turned away from this love. Why on earth would they do that, one might ask? Distrust. As soon as the Serpent promised them wisdom rather than death they didn't trust God anymore. In their limited experience they had never seen him fight for them, never seen him prove himself. They had never known anything but contentment and happiness. But now the Serpent tells them there is something they haven't seen, something God is keeping from them. How dare he! Didn't he set them to rule over all creation? Then why can't they rule over this tree as well? Their desire for self-determination grows and the fruit becomes irresistible. Because they didn't trust that whatever God was keeping from them would maybe be better not to have.

So eating from the Tree of Knowledge of Good and Evil is Man's vote of no-confidence in God. Even though we were made to love him and be loved by him, we run from the relationship we were meant to live in, because we don't trust him. And love without trust is impossible. Oh, but God still wants to be able to love us and for us to be able to love him. So what is he to do now? How can he teach us the way back to him, now that we have run away and become our own demise? He does it by revealing himself, by making himself known to us as the one true source of all security, provision, and fulfilment, so that we might understand the true meaning of freedom in him.

How does God do it?

My Dad always used to say: "You can parent your kids all you want, they will imitate you anyway." What just seemed to be one of those casual sayings when I was growing up, holds quite a bit of godly principle. We learn by watching our parents rather than by listening to them. Because love doesn't talk, preach, and claim; love does. So God shows himself by giving an elaborate, indisputable example. He stages a great rescue, revealing himself as our redeemer. He follows it up with a string of miracles, revealing himself as our provider. And then, most wonderful of all, he establishes a place for us and him to be close once again, revealing himself as our fulfilment.

I am talking about the story of Exodus, Israel's deliverance from Egypt. It is THE story of freedom, but it is also a great revelation of who God is, how he loves us, and what our relationship with him could be. If we look at the story from God's perspective, every step from slavery into the Promised Land is God presenting himself. He had to suffer through Man turning away from him in distrust, so now he wants to make himself known to us. He wants to be our God again, our only source of redemption, provision, and fulfilment. To show us what and who he is, he gives this great example: His story with Israel, his chosen people.

At least they are called the Chosen People. When we look a bit closer, though, it becomes apparent that they are actually a created people. It starts when God reveals himself to Abraham in Genesis 12:1-2.

The Lord said to Abram, "Go from your country, your people and your father's household to the land I will show you. I will make you into a great nation, and I will bless you; I will make your name great, and you will be a blessing."

At the time of Abraham's first encounter with God he is 75 and childless. So God's promise might not have made much sense to him. But this encounter changes Abrahams life and he obeys immediately. God repeats his promise to Abraham several times, and over two decades later and against all odds and despite her age his wife Sarah finally has a son, Isaac. It seems weird that God would choose an infertile family to start a people. It was not only Sarah who had a miraculous pregnancy, Rebekah was also barren until Isaac prayed for her, and so was Rachel. This feels like God wanted his hand in this whole story from the very beginning. God did not choose an existing people, he created one from scratch. And why? To be their God.

"I will establish my covenant as an everlasting covenant between me and you and your descendants after you for the generations to come, to be your God and the God of your descendants after you."
(Genesis 17:7)

He wants a people to reveal himself to as the almighty God. He makes a covenant with Abraham and also reveals his plan to him:

"Know for certain that for four hundred years your descendants will be strangers in a country not their own and that they will be enslaved and mistreated there. But I will punish the nation they serve as slaves, and afterward they will come out with great possessions." (Genesis 15: 13-14)

God planned this whole thing several hundred years in advance. He planned for Israel and his sons to settle in Egypt and for their descendants to become slaves, for he planned to reveal himself to them as the God who delivers, provides, and fulfils. He set his great story of deliverance in motion when he chose Abraham. And he wants the story to last, to never be forgotten. That is why he decrees the Feast of Passover to be celebrated every year in remembrance of his great deeds in Exodus 12: 1-20, and to this day his people do so as if they had been there themselves. It is so important to him that he tells them to commemorate something that is only just about to happen. And afterwards he calls himself "The Lord your God who brought you out of Egypt" (for example in Exodus 20:2), because he identifies himself so much with this great story. It simply must be of lasting importance.

The 15 steps into perfect freedom

It is no wonder that it takes Israel quite a number of years to get out of slavery into Gods perfect freedom. It is quite a road to take. Following the 15 verses of the Dayenu, it takes the Children of Israel 15 distinct steps from slavery into the Promised Land, every single one of them a miracle in its own right.

Here is how to this day every Jewish family remembers and celebrates their ancestors' amazing journey into God's freedom on Passover, just as if they themselves had lived through it as well:

If He had brought us out of Egypt, and not carried out judgment against them
Dayenu, it would have been enough!

If He had carried out judgment against them, and not against their idols
Dayenu, it would have been enough!

If He had destroyed their idols, and had not slain their first-born
Dayenu, it would have been enough!

If He had slain their firstborn, and had not given us their wealth
Dayenu, it would have been enough!

If He had given us their wealth, and had not split the sea for us
Dayenu, it would have been enough!

If He had split the sea for us, and had not taken us through it on dry land
Dayenu, it would have been enough!

If He had taken us through the sea on dry land, and had not drowned our oppressors in it
Dayenu, it would have been enough!

If He had drowned our oppressors in it, and had not supplied for our needs in the desert for forty years
Dayenu, it would have been enough!

If He had supplied for our needs in the desert for forty years, and had not fed us the manna
Dayenu, it would have been enough!

If He had fed us manna, and had not given us the Shabbat
Dayenu, it would have been enough!

If He had given us the Shabbat, and had not brought us before Mount Sinai
Dayenu, it would have been enough!

If He had brought us before Mount Sinai, and had not given us the Torah
Dayenu, it would have been enough!

If He had given us the Torah, and had not brought us into the land of Israel
Dayenu, it would have been enough!

If He had brought us into the land of Israel, and not built for us the Holy Temple
Dayenu, it would have been enough!

Every verse tells of a moment of revelation, with every step God makes himself known to us. We can find God's character revealed, see his grace portrayed, and his mode of operation displayed. So that we might know and trust him enough to step into his perfect freedom, even if that means to be dependent on him and not be our own masters anymore.

Deliverance Enough

The Five Stanzas of Leaving Slavery

The first five stanzas of the Dayenu reveal God as the mighty deliverer. They are the five steps he takes to break us free from our sin and oppression. The five revelations it takes for us to realize that true security and safety is only found in him. And once again his deliverance doesn't start with the Exodus but actually 80 years before, this time with a wicker basket.

The courageous and loving act of his desperate mother saves Moses from Pharaoh's killing order, allows him to be saved by Pharaoh's daughter, and enables him to be the only Hebrew to grow up a free man. He enjoys all the privileges the king's court has to offer and receives the ideal education to become a leader for his people. Then, at 40 years old, fear and scandal drive him away from his homeland and the following 40 years as a shepherd among strangers make him more humble than ever before. Thus he finds the burning bush. Thus he encounters the God of his forefathers for the very first time.

This encounter must have shaken Moses to his very core. Right in the middle of the desert he steps onto holy ground, hears the voice of the God of Abraham, Isaac, and Jacob, and on top of that is instructed to lead Israel out of Egypt. No wonder he had questions. What did he know? Nothing. Not even the name of the god he was talking to.

Through his Egyptian education Moses must have known several hundred, if not thousands of gods. Each one with a specific name and field of work. So, it was only natural for Moses to ask God his name, because the name would bring clarity by shedding light on accompanying powers, responsibilities, and areas of expertise. I suppose, God's answer was far from satisfactory. He simply says one word. We usually translate it as "I am", but while "I am" defines the word as present tense the Hebrew doesn't have a tense at all. Which could be translated to "I was, am, and will be", "I am eternal" or even "I exist".

I love this passage. I love how God just won't let Moses get away with his attempts of classification. Instead, he explains with just one word: He cannot be put into words. He cannot be defined by expertise or responsibilities. He is responsible for everything. He cannot be labelled. He is above any description. Moses has no choice but to get to know God as he is.

That is the difference between the God of Israel and all other gods and idols of mankind. This makes the difference between faith and religion. With his name alone God expresses his desire for relationship. He wants to be known. His name clarifies that he exists, is alive, is tangible. And it invites us to step closer, dive deeper, and discover more than meets the eye.

God deliberately does NOT say: "I am the Almighty, I am the Omniscient". He says: "I am what I am. You'll have to come and explore me. Come and discover my character. Come closer and experience me."

I love that! God is who he is and wants to be experienced. And every encounter with him invites me, entices me to advance further into his character, to deepen our relationship, and to fall more and more in love with him. He made us for this deep relationship. The indescribability, the inconceivability of God's being is found in us as well. For we are part of him and only complete in him. And only in relationship with him can we truly answer the question of his name. Only in relationship with him can we find who we truly are.

If He had brought us out of Egypt

Right after his invitation to get to know him, God starts the greatest display of his power, his heart, his faithfulness, and his mercy. For the entire world to see he extends his arm and proves himself as the almighty saviour.

"I have seen the misery of my people in Egypt. I have heard them crying out because of their slave drivers, and I am concerned about their suffering. So I have come down to rescue them from the hand of the Egyptians and to bring them into a good and spacious land, flowing with milk and honey."(Exodus 3:7+8)

That is the first step into freedom: God answering. He not only heard their cry but was moved by it. And while he announces his intention to intervene, he also gives a glimpse of what the life he wants to give them will be like. It will be a land of milk and honey, a place of security and provision. The land God describes couldn't be further from what his people know life to be like so far. What a great exchange this would be!

"The cry of the Israelites has reached me", God says next. "I have seen the way the Egyptians are oppressing them. So now, go. I am sending you to Pharaoh to bring my people, the Israelites, out of Egypt." (Exodus 3:9+10)

It seems very simple. One command: Go and bring them out of Egypt. Tell Pharaoh to comply. Easy, right? Well, if it was anyone but God saying this, it would seem quite ridiculous. But if the almighty God is determined to intervene, it is anything but laughable. At least, that is obvious to us. Moses, however, seems to have some doubts.

"What if the Children of Israel don't believe me?" he asks God. "How will they know you sent me?" And God is not above proving himself. He gives Moses miracles to perform. He tells him to throw his staff on the ground, which turns into a snake, and to put his hands into the folds of his cloak, which is leprous when he takes it out again.

"If they do not believe you or pay attention to the first sign, they may believe the second. But if they do not believe these two signs or listen to you, take some water from the Nile and pour it on the dry ground. It will become blood." (Exodus 4:8+9)

Moses is still timid at this point. He, again, asks God to send someone else, because he deems himself not a great speaker. And now God has had enough of this, he angrily agrees to send him Aaron, Moses' brother, to do the talking, leaving Moses without any argument. The three miracles must suffice to show God's might to his people and validate Moses' calling as a godsend leader. And it works. Moses performs the signs before the people of Israel

'and they believed. And when they heard that the Lord was concerned about them and had seen their misery, they bowed down and worshipped.'(Exodus 4:31)

That is just how God comes to rescue us. He finds us right where we are, crying out to him in our shackles. He answers our cries, giving us an undeniable revelation of him as the source of security and provision. And if we just cannot believe, he gives us signs and miracles, to prove his existence and love for us beyond all doubt. At least, that is what I have seen in many a conversion story.

Laura[3] was a patient in a psychiatric clinic, suffering from burnout, when she reached a tipping point. The treatment wasn't helping, she was overwhelmed by the emotional trauma she was forced to face for the first time in her life. The pain had become unbearable. Determined to commit suicide, she cried to God one last time: "If you exist and want me to live, do something to show me. Otherwise I will end this here and now."

She meant it. Was already holding a hairdryer, ready to get into the bathtub and electrocute herself. Her cry came from the heart, and it moved God to intervene. Seconds later several people burst into her room, two friends and an orderly. All three shouting her name, because they all had had a sudden feeling: something was wrong with Laura. Her life was saved that day. And this was only the first of several undeniable encounters with God. She started to ask God questions and he immediately sent people her way who would answer them. She would sometimes fall asleep with a problem on her mind and wake up with the impulse to look up something specific on the internet that didn't seem to relate to the problem at all, but somehow held the solution anyway. Her life was changed by that first rousing encounter with God, and ever since then she has followed him with a childlike faith, trusting him to answer her cry with miracles, security, and provision, be it in her marriage, her business, or her ministry.

Matthew was extremely sceptical towards religion in general when his mother started telling him about her newfound faith in Jesus. He was glad she was happy, but he wanted nothing to do with it. So, when she asked him

---

[3] All names in this book were altered for anonymity purposes.

to accompany her to a church service, he only complied because she had just broken her arm and couldn't drive herself. Not wanting to sit and wait in the car by himself, he sat in church with his arms crossed and his heart hardened. If God existed, which he seriously doubted, he would be neither nice nor powerful, Matthew thought, full of bitterness. Because a nice and powerful God wouldn't have let it happen that his Dad had left the family, crushing Matthew's trust in father figures everywhere. So these people around him were clearly delusional.

But then God showed himself by healing Matthew's mother's arm right there and then. The pain was gone, her movement fully restored, and when she stormed to the doctor's the next day to tell him to remove the screws in her arm four weeks too early, the doctor had to break them free from the bone that had regrown so rapidly. Matthew was shocked; the door to his heart had been kicked in. Now it was open to encounter the Heavenly Father and begin a journey towards healing, new purpose, and a loving family of his own.

Carol's encounter happened on a retreat of self-improvement through life-coaching. She had been handed a stack of index cards by the coach and was sent off into the woods. This was supposed to be a sort of guided pilgrim's journey. Each card contained thoughts and questions about nature, the being behind creation, and the purpose of it all. The first couple of index cards inspired Carol to enjoy the view, the fresh air, and the beauty surrounding her. The following card simply said: "If there is a God behind all this, what do you suppose he is like?"

Carol mused about this for some time and then had the impulse to just ask: "If you exist, show me what you are like." Right at that moment a deer stalked out of the undergrowth and stopped in its tracks only a few metres away from her. To Carol that was a moving encounter and an answer at the same time. To her the image of a deer had always been a symbol for tenderness, mildness, and harmony; almost the polar opposite of what she feared God might be like. She couldn't believe it; the deer stood still and stared at her for almost ten minutes before turning and walking away. Carol felt dizzy. Continuing her walk she read the next cards and on one of them the suggestion: "Now you can ask God what he thinks of you." She kept walking while she asked God, but immediately had to stop in her tracks, because right in the middle of the trail was her answer: A beautiful heart-shaped stone. With a tiny remnant of doubt she looked around to see if maybe all rocks here were shaped like hearts. None of them were; on the contrary, all the other rocks were craggy and rough with sharp edges. Only this one beautiful heart, placed right in front of her, was smooth and round. Almost as if God had let it fall from heaven just for her.

I could go on and on, telling stories just like that about the moment where God intervened and answered the cries of people with rousing encounters, signs, and miracles. He is still not above proving himself, he is still moved, is still concerned about our sufferings. He doesn't allow even a shred of doubt that it is actually him we meet. And he still, right in that first moment, gives us a glimpse of what a life with him will be like.

So, if you are unsure whether or not God is real, feel free to ask him to show himself to you. He is more than willing to have a rousing encounter with you. And if you are in doubt whether or not he is worth following, ask him to prove himself to you. He is more than willing to send signs and wonders for you to realise how much he loves you. And don't talk yourself out of believing in him. Hold on to that first initial overwhelming realisation of God's existence, to the first love he showed you in that first rousing encounter.

Maybe you feel like God might be angry because, just like Moses, you haggled for more and more proof instead of following him. If that is you, trust me: it is okay to say sorry. Don't stay stuck in your doubt and the false entitlement to yet another miracle. You can turn and thank God for the proof he already gave you. I have learned over the years: None of my stupidities, none of my rebellion, none of my past, present and future sins shock God in the slightest. When I turn from them and to him and ask for an encounter, he always, always, always happily answers my plea.

So, maybe it's time for you to find out whether or not God is for real. Just go and ask him for an encounter. Maybe you long for solid confirmation whether or not he truly loves you and wants to rescue you from your Egypt. Just go and ask him for your three signs. And maybe you feel sorry you never really reacted to God's initial first encounter and wonder whether or not he is still in, whether or not he still wants you. Just go ask him for forgiveness.

It's just one small prayer that will make a whole lot of difference in your life and your relationship with the Heavenly Father. You won't need special words, an altar, a priest, or a church to do so. Just say it. Tell God what you hope for.

"I long to know you as the I AM. I want to be sure you have come for me and love me. I am sorry I didn't follow you before, even though you have proven yourself to me already. Now I want to see you truly rescue me from my oppression."

He will jump at the chance to answer you. He can't wait to bring you back to himself. He is who he was, who he is, and who he will be. He spared nothing to save his people, he will spare nothing to save you.

If he had carried out judgement against them

Immediately after God has ordered Moses to go bring the Israelites out of Egypt he tells him:

"When you return to Egypt, see that you perform before Pharaoh all the wonders I have given you the power to do. But I will harden his heart so that he will not let the people go." (Exodus 4:21)

Now, that just seems unnecessarily complicated. If the Almighty wants his people out of there, why not soften Pharaoh's heart rather than harden it? That would make things easier, right? But apparently God did not set out for easy, maybe because his perfect freedom takes a little more than just walking out of your oppression. He is determined to save completely, body, mind, and soul. That takes more than one step. Because for his people to be free, God not only needs to take them out of slavery, but also needs to take the slave out of them. Israel needs to see how wrong the worldview, beliefs, and sense of self are that living in slavery has forced on them. They need to realise that the only civilisation they know so far is not worth copying and doesn't please him at all. They need to understand this before they involve themselves with God. They need to know, they mustn't stay part of this culture, mustn't believe the lies and insecurities slavery has fed to them. God raining judgement on Egypt sets the record straight about what is true and what is abhorrent to him.

Apart from Pharaoh's hardened heart Moses faces another problem when he tries to follow God's orders. The people, who were excited by the miracles and the prospect of freedom at first, quickly turn against him. After being told by Moses to let God's people go Pharaoh lets the Israelites suffer his wrath, making their workload unbearable by forcing them to find their own supplies. And since this whole injustice started with Moses showing up, rattling Pharaoh's cage, they make him responsible for it. They become angry with him for complicating everything with the Egyptians, and say all had been fine before Moses came and made a mess of the whole slavery situation. Later on, in the desert, they would repeat their cries and declare they wish they were still back in Egypt.

Oppression has left its mark on the Israelites. They have grown accustomed to it to a certain extent. They are in denial about the severity of it. For them to even want to be freed, they need to truly grasp the seriousness of their own situation. It might at first look like God is making things worse for the Israelites to force them out of Egypt, which could be construed as cruel. But the problem is not the workload and denied supply. The problem is Israel being completely at Pharaoh's mercy. He can decide whether they live or die, he holds all the cards. That is what they were in denial about. That is what God needed them to see. Because that is from which he wants to free them.

So, neither the Egyptians nor the Israelites get an easy out. Instead God shows himself as the only god mighty to save and deliver. The Egyptians, too, get the great opportunity to see him as he is. Both peoples learn they put their trust in false gods. Both encounter the only source of true security. And by raining judgement on Egypt God unmasks Israel's oppressors and forces them to show their true colours. Slowly and almost begrudgingly the Children of Israel realize, they really need to get away and leave the life of slavery behind. For centuries they had known nothing but servitude. But now God opens their eyes and they realize: this situation truly is unbearable; we need to get out of here.

Just like the Israelites we often have a very hard time understanding how enslaved we really are. We, too, have grown accustomed to our own situation and are in denial about the true state of affairs. We even cherish our slavery to a certain extend. We know our way around by now, find security in the walls holding us captive. So just like his people we often react to his rescue plan by back-pedalling. "Oh no, God, you misunderstood. I just wanted to have it a little more comfortable, a little less burdened. No need to leave this lovely country. Just get the Egyptians a little off my back, that's all I'm asking for."

But that would not be God's true, lasting freedom, would it? So, God needs and wants to show us how oppressing our situation really is. And the best way to expose the oppression masking as a not so bad, just a little uncomfortable life is to rain judgment on it. Put it into perspective. Show us how terrible and destructive the life we have gotten used to truly is. This can be a very painful process. But it is just what we need. Because God cannot free us from something we don't even perceive as oppressing. So, our oppression must be unmasked and revealed for what it is.

Also, we need to see him as different to what we know so far. We need to grasp how he is nothing like the life we know, nothing like the masters we are familiar with. We need to understand that we mustn't stay in the civilisation and culture we grew up in. We need for him to open our eyes to the devastating state of our lives. We need his light to shine right through our darkness to realise: this situation truly is unbearable, we need to get out of here!

But how do we react to this revelation? Usually the same way the Israelites did. Angry, confused, trying to blame someone. "Hey God, this doesn't feel like freedom. I wanted you to save me, not come here and make everything worse. All was well before you showed up and totally ruined my slavery!" Or, if we already understand God's perfect goodness and cannot bring ourselves to blame him, it must be the enemy trying to bring us down and God apparently abandoning us in our time of need. Both reactions are wrong and, what is worse, keep us from God's true freedom. If I choose to stay in denial I say no to the truth and no to God's deliverance. If I mistake God's rain of judgment on my oppressors for an attack I will probably not humble myself and seek God's freedom.

God does not rain judgment on *us*. He doesn't want to shock us or bully us into anything. He merely shows us all the facts we had been suppressing so expertly before. And with this revelation of the sometimes very ugly truth comes his offer of freedom. His invitation to let him rescue us from our oppressors.

I have seen and experienced several ways of this rain of judgment. Sometimes it is just a grand realisation of the true state of affairs. As if God would just turn off all ability to endure. It was like that for my friend Eliza. Several counsellors and friends had already told her she needed to change her oppressive living situation to change her life.

"But why would I?" she asked me. "I am comfortable, I have everything I need, all is good."

I couldn't believe what I was hearing. Almost nothing in her life would I have described as good. It was shocking to find she didn't see it. In desperation I said: "Well, then all

I can do is to pray for God to show you how bad your circumstances truly are."

A couple of months later Eliza and I talked on the phone and when I asked her how she had been, she almost blurted out: "I feel terrible. Because you prayed I cannot stand being here anymore! It is unbearable to live like this, nothing is good! I want out of here!"

It sounded like she blamed me for her insufferable circumstances, but if it hadn't been for this realisation, Eliza would not have opened her heart to God's deliverance. She would not have, for the first time in her life, travelled on her own only three months later. And she would not have moved abroad for a year, and maybe would not have gone to university after that.

At other times God's rain of judgement happens as a reaction to our longing to be closer to him. Because in order to come closer it is sometimes necessary to let go of the things that keep me from him. His judgement helps me realise which of my behaviours or habits is actually oppressing me, so that I might let go and instead step into true closeness with him. I remember one time we were having a youth group worship service, the Holy Spirit was clearly moving in the congregation, and the atmosphere was thick with God's love. Yet I couldn't feel it at all. I tried everything, singing louder, praying harder, nothing worked. So I asked God what was going on. Why couldn't I experience his obvious presence?

"Because your heart is hardened. You protect yourself by letting nothing move you, so I can't either."

His answer left me in shock. I had never wanted to keep him out. So, when I got home that night, I threw myself on the bed and cried for what felt like several hours. I begged God to give me a heart of flesh again in exchange for the stone I had turned mine into. After a long time of desperate sobbing the Holy Spirit moved and I felt peace come over me. So I got up, brushed my teeth, and went to sleep. In the weeks following that night I realised a change in me on numerous occasions. Whenever I watched a heart-warming movie, I didn't need to make jokes anymore but instead could just be moved by it. Sometimes to tears. And in situations that normally would have hurt me I felt I didn't need to protect myself anymore because God stepped in as my protector. Nothing was overwhelming anymore, I could freely feel emotions, because God was my protection and my comfort now.

But if a mere realisation is not enough, I need to be shaken up quite a bit, before I can fully grasp the severity of the oppression I have gotten used to. This usually happens by things going horribly wrong until my back is against the wall. Once I was almost fired from a job because I was a slave to a crippling lie, severely limiting my ability to succeed. My boss had called me in for an evaluation and got more and more desperate with me, because she just couldn't understand why I was such an underachiever.

"You have so many gifts, such potential. Why aren't you using any of it? Can't you see that you are gifted? Don't you see yourself as talented?"

What she didn't know was that, while she was giving vent to her desperation, there was a dialog going on in my mind. My soul was screaming 'Of course I am NOT talented in the least! I have nothing to give, nothing!' while my spirit was talking to God. 'I know this is a lie. A lie I have confessed to believing many a time. I have asked you to establish your truth in me. Why can I still not believe you have gifted me?' 'Because you need to hear it from your father. He never told you what talents he sees in you. His silence cemented this lie in you, his endorsement is going to break it.'

So, that night I drove two hours to my parents' house to hear my father tell me I am gifted. And because God is God, this conversation did not only set *me* free but my father as well.

This process of judgement and realisation of my oppression can cost many a tear, can be painful and exhausting. But you know what it always is? Liberating beyond measure. I can finally let go and watch my saviour save me. This could never happen if I'd keep believing my life to be kind of okay and not too bad. I need his rain of judgement to finally understand the state I'm in, and then I need his saving. And he always comes through for me. Always.

So, how about you? Did you ever find yourself in situations where your circumstances became unbearable all of a sudden, without you really knowing why? Do you remember moments in your life where you were shocked to find how enslaved you really are? Or do you wonder right now whether or not you might be enslaved, but are just too content with your familiar oppression?

Then don't fall into the trap of misjudging your situation. Don't mistake God's invitation to give you his perfect freedom as an evil attack. He longs to reveal himself to you as the true source of security, provision, and fulfilment. But in order to show you how much he wants you, you have to realise how much you need him.

So, maybe it's time to see the great chance your unbearable circumstances offer you: to encounter God as you have never seen him before. Maybe use the realisation of your dire need for a saviour to reach out for God to rescue you. Maybe ask God whether you are too content with your oppression. Maybe it's time to step out of the civilisation you have grown into and ask God to take the slave out of you to take you out of slavery. Again, a short, unceremonious prayer will make the difference. Just a small but heartfelt reaction to God's revelation.

"In all my terrible circumstances I want to encounter you as I have never seen you before. I cannot bear my oppression anymore, please reveal yourself to me as my redeemer. Show me where I am too content with my circumstances and help me to leave the civilisation I have grown into behind. Please take the slave out of me to take me out of slavery."

God will gladly reveal himself to you. For he loves you to know him as he truly is: your saviour and your redeemer.

If he had destroyed their idols

After showing his people how enslaved they truly are and how much they need him to rescue them, God takes the next step. To break them free from the clutches of their oppressors, he unleashes ten plagues upon Egypt, each one more terrifying than the last. The river that made the lands fruitful is turned into a deathly puddle of blood. The crops are eaten by grasshoppers. A large portion of the cattle dies. Frogs, mosquitoes, lice, and rashes plague the Egyptians. Huge hailstones destroy the country. The sun turns dark, and death comes to every family. Every aspect of Egyptian life gets devastated. While Goshen, where the Hebrews live, remains untouched, the rest of Egypt is laid to waste, and their gods stay quiet. Again and again Pharaoh has to beg Moses to call upon his God for Egypt's sake. He gets so desperate, he promises to let the Israelites go, if only the plagues would stop, just to change his mind again later. So another plague comes, and another, and another, to bring Pharaoh to his knees, to finally make him let God's people go.

Or so it would seem. Oftentimes the plagues are construed as the necessary measures to force Pharaoh into releasing Israel. In most retellings or dramatizations he gets portrayed as prideful and stubborn, he apparently needs to be broken. This cannot be what the plagues are for, though. God himself told Moses beforehand and more than once: HE will harden Pharaoh's heart. He will MAKE Pharaoh not want to let Israel go. Which can only mean that Pharaoh probably would have cracked sooner, would have given in earlier, hadn't it been for God's interference. So why does God go to such lengths? If he didn't need the plagues to force Pharaoh's hand, why send them at all? He must have had a greater, deeper purpose for bringing such terrors upon Egypt. If he didn't actually need to break Israel free from the clutches of the Egyptians, whose clutches were the plagues for then?

In Exodus 12:12 God gives Moses the answer to this question:

"I will bring judgment on all the gods of Egypt. I am the I AM."

That is the purpose of the plagues. They are not a show of force, nor a necessity to break Pharaoh. They are a show of God's power and sovereignty. He wants to unmask the Egyptian gods as false idols. And he wants to show himself not only as an almighty rescuer but also as the only true God. Egypt's gods can do nothing to stop the destruction, no matter how much Pharaoh's priests and magicians cry out to them. Each plague must have been a crushing blow for the Egyptians. They had gods specializing in every area of life and none of them can do anything about the destruction. None of them interfere, none of them save Egypt. Having to deal with the plague itself is one thing. But also having to cope with being betrayed and abandoned by the gods they had put their trust in? That must have been utterly disastrous and mortifying. Their idols can offer neither security nor provision in this onslaught. One by one they all get dismantled and humiliated, uncovered as powerless.

God wants Israel to see and know that. He wants them to realise that he alone is God and none of the Egyptian idols are worth worshipping. He wants to break his people free from the clutches of the only deities they've known so far. He wants to free them from putting their trust into false gods. Israel and Egypt alike get to witness God's power and superiority and see God displayed as almighty, sovereign, and the only real deal, the only true source of security and provision.

We, too, need to be freed from the clutches of our oppressors. We, too, need to see our false gods to be incapable of offering security and provision. But what idols are we talking about here? To be honest, the notion of idolatry was always a little hard to grasp for me. Apart from decorative Buddha figurines I have never seen any idols in my life. Growing up in post-enlightenment Europe there were no temples, no altars, no statues of any gods in my life, except of course in museums. And whenever idolatry was discussed in Sunday school, there seemed to be no real understanding of it, even among the grown-ups.

"Well, your television or you hobby can be a false god", was usually the only explanation we got back then. This statement made it seem like idols are things that take up my time and maybe derail my focus away from God. Which in turn had me thinking that God wanted everyone to lead the life of a hermit, where nothing but prayer was the order of the day, because everything else would be idolatry. That seems impractical and unattainable. Especially when back then school was taking up most of my time. I just couldn't see school as being my idol.

To understand what idols really are, it is better to look at what God is and what we lost because of the Fall. We are made to be God's friends. Made to be in a close relationship with him, to be dependent on him, to be incomplete without him. We have a hole in our soul as infinite as God himself and only his fullness can satisfy it. Without God we need to find security and protection elsewhere, we need to find provision elsewhere, we need to find fulfilment elsewhere. So when we turned from

God, we immediately started to use our newfound self-determination to find substitutes to try and fill that hole by any means necessary. Looking at the known polytheistic cultures and religions in history we see that humankind was always looking for the same things when worshipping any deity: Protect me, provide for me, give my life fulfilment with meaning, purpose, happiness, and hope of eternity. Egypt worshipped the river that brought fruitfulness and wealth. They worshipped cattle as the embodiment of their riches. They worshipped the sun that brought life. They worshipped gods of healing and resurrection. Those were the gods Israel knew so far; until God mightily proved himself to be the one and only true source of all security, provision, and fulfilment.

To this day we seek to find fullness to feel whole. To this day we have this infinite hole in our souls. False securities, false provision, and false fulfilment we try to cram into it. So this hole is pretty stuffed when God finds us in our own personal Egypt. And if he wants to give us his fullness, he first needs to clear out the substitutes. Anything we put our trust in stands in the way of knowing God as our security. Anything we expect sustainment from stands in the way of knowing God as our provision. Anything we seek purpose, meaning, happiness, and hope of eternity from stands in the way of knowing God as our fulfilment.

For a long time I trusted sarcasm, dark humour, and judging people to protect my heart from pain. That was my false security, my idol. I wore it like a shield and used it like a sword. It worked very well until I got so hard-hearted and emotionally distant that I couldn't experience God's closeness anymore. God unmasked my idol as my true oppressor by revealing how incapable and powerless this false god was. Instead of saving me from pain, it had shackled me and I was starving behind my own emotional walls. To be freed, I had to let go of this armour of self-protection and blindly trust that God would be the protector he had promised me to be.

Elisabeth, growing up in an oppressive family of co-dependent relationships, had learned she needed to stay alert and always prepared to defuse any situation with the potential to escalate. Constantly in need to navigate emotionally abusive attacks, foresight, appeasement, and an excessive sense of responsibility became her idols. Which shackled her to condemnation and shame, and left her exhausted in constant fear for her life. One by one, God addressed these issues, showed Elisabeth that he is different, caring, peaceful, and never oppressive; until she trusted him enough to let go of her system of safety, and started to walk in the new life with him as her protector.

Richard was being treated for burnout and severe panic attacks when he realised he was worshipping financial stability and social standing as the gods he expected security from. Though he was a well-respected, wealthy man, he lived in constant fear his company would go bankrupt and his reputation and image in society would be destroyed. The astonishing thing was: he wasn't even head of said company anymore. His son had taken over years before, when Richard retired. Still, his self-worth and sense of security were entirely and irrevocably linked to its success. So, when God showed him his true value and security in him, Richard's life changed dramatically. Turning from his old idols and to the true source of safety and provision freed him from panic attacks and gave him new strength and purpose.

Letting go of these false securities is often a leap of faith. Because if I let go of what has kept me from being harmed and hurt, I am for a moment unprotected and that is scary. It might even feel life-threatening. But God is patient with us. To lead me into his deep running freedom he lovingly reveals not only my oppression to me, but my substitutes for his fullness: My false gods, my idols, my false securities, my self-protection, and everything I used to fill that God-shaped hole in my soul. All the things I thought I needed to survive are put into perspective. So I can realise how they brought me death instead. What happens when we turn to God to fill this hole is written in Isaiah 61:1-3. Good news to the poor, bandages for the broken-hearted, freedom for the captives and release from darkness for the prisoners, comfort to all who mourn, a crown of beauty instead of ashes, the oil of joy instead of mourning, and praise instead of a spirit of despair. Everything gets exchanged for something infinitely better: the fullness of God.

So, what do you think clutters up the God-shaped hole in your soul? Who or what do you turn to for security, provision, and fulfilment? Maybe you know exactly in what area of your life you put your trust in something other than God. Maybe your search for security, provision, and fulfilment drove you to do some pretty sinful things and established some pretty destructive habits. Maybe God is shaking up your life right now to unmask and dismantle your false securities before your eyes. No matter where you stand in this process, one thing is absolutely certain: God will save you, provide for you, and fulfil you, if you let him. Neither sin, nor shame, nor idolatry will keep God from coming to your rescue. All you have to do is ask.

"I know I have looked to false gods for security, provision, and fulfilment. I tried to fil my soul with things that left me broken, bound, and shackled. Now I see how wrong it was, now I know true freedom is only found in you. Please come and release me from these shackles of my own doing. From now on I will trust in you to be my redeemer, my provider, and the source of my fulfilment."

You will see, anything you offer God on the altar, anything you give up, will be exchanged for something infinitely better: the fullness of God.

If he had slain the firstborn

Nine plagues have come and gone. Nine times idols were unmasked and humiliated. Nine times Egypt was shattered while Goshen remained untouched by the horrors that befell the lands. Eight times Pharaoh asked Moses to pray to God on his behalf, promising Israel's freedom in exchange. Eight times God hardened Pharaoh's heart so he would not let Israel go.

The tenth plague is different, however. It will be the very last time God brings judgement upon Egypt's idols. After this, God tells Moses, Pharaoh will not only let them go but drive them out of the country, so they have to prepare for departure.

> *"About midnight I will go throughout Egypt. Every firstborn son in Egypt will die, from the firstborn son of Pharaoh, who sits on the throne, to the firstborn son of the female slave, who is at her hand mill, and all the firstborn of the cattle as well."*
> *(Exodus 11: 4+5)*

"This month is to be for you the first month, the first month of your year. Tell the whole community of Israel that on the tenth day of this month each man is to take a lamb for his family, one for each household[…] and slaughter them at twilight. […]This is how you are to eat it: with your cloak tucked into your belt, your sandals on your feet and your staff in your hand. Eat it in haste; it is the Lord's Passover. On that same night I will pass through Egypt and strike down every firstborn of both people and animals, and I will bring judgment on all the gods of Egypt. I am the I AM. The blood will be a sign for you on the houses where you are, and when I see the blood, I will pass over you. No destructive plague will touch you when I strike Egypt. This is a day you are to commemorate; for

the generations to come you shall celebrate it as a festival to the Lord—a lasting ordinance." (Exodus 12:2-6 + 11-14)

This last blow to free his people is a matter of life and death for Israel and their oppressors alike. This time the plague will hit both camps, if they don't prepare for it according to God's orders. He gives very clear instructions how to be spared from this most terrible of all the plagues. And with these instructions he also decrees: his people shall from now on commemorate this day in celebration of their deliverance. In every Hebrew household a lamb must be slaughtered at twilight and its blood smeared on the doorframes. The blood will be a sign for this house to be spared by God.

But why is this time different than the nine before? Why do they have to make an effort to be spared this time? Why need there be bloodshed in every house? And why is this event so important to God that he orders the Israelites to remember it while it is happening? It must be of special significance to God's rescue plan. It can't be just to humiliate the Egyptian god of death, because this time Pharaoh doesn't have to go and ask the God of Israel for help. This plague doesn't seem to be to put pressure on Egypt, rather, it feels like it needs to happen. While the other idols needed to be unmasked, because worshipping them would be misdirected and therefore disappointed hope, the god of death seems to have a just claim on Israel. A claim that needs to be broken with blood. Is that God's purpose for this whole ordeal?

On that Seder evening in my parents' house, after the Holy Spirit had given me this revelation and after all the guests had gone, I was bubbling over with excitement. Mom, Dad, and I were in the kitchen cleaning up, while I enthusiastically chatted away, telling them what I had just realized during the reading of the Dayenu. For every verse I could instantly name an example from my life to show how this is still the way God saves us and draws us back to him. For every verse but this one. In my excitement I just skipped it and talked about the others instead. Two years later, when I first tried to put this revelation into words, I got stuck on that verse again. I still couldn't see the role the tenth plague played in God's rescue plan. Why kill the firstborn? What was that about?

The Holy Spirit answered me with a question: "Well, who is God's firstborn that was killed?" And again, this question came down like a sword and opened a thick book of truth in my mind. Of course! This plague alludes to Jesus! It is not about unmasking the Egyptian god of death as powerless, but about overcoming death itself! The death of the first-born is the most important plague of them all, because it shows God as the conqueror of death. The same death every living human being deserves for their sins. So, this plague cannot pass Israel by, because each and every one of them needs to be freed from eternal damnation. This is how far God's freedom goes: Freedom from death, from eternal separation from God. It is the blood of the lamb, the blood of the firstborn that restores the relationship with God to what it was in Eden. This is why God took it upon himself to harden the heart of Pharaoh. Because it wasn't enough to free his people from Egypt, with body, mind, and soul. He wanted to free them from death itself, wanted them to be free to step back into the loving, fulfilling relationship with the Heavenly Father.

To overcome death blood needs to be spilled. It's not enough to leave slavery and false gods behind. To be truly free, the death sentence sin brought upon Man needs to be reversed. And God does that by stepping in himself. Because he became Man and spilled his own blood, ours could be spared. By painting their doors with the blood of the Passover lamb the Israelites proclaim the victory of the lamb to come, Jesus.

This plague brings the Children of Israel to a crossroads. For the first time since God revealed himself to Moses they are forced to act. If they want the tenth plague to pass them by, they need to do something about it. They need to actively step into God's covenant by obeying and following his orders. They need to take this step themselves, need to decide for themselves whether or not they want to follow God. Whether or not they want to be freed from eternal damnation. It is their decision to make. It is their own hands that smear the blood onto their doorframes. Their own resolve to proclaim the victory of the lamb to come.

Likewise, God doesn't stop at freeing me from oppression with body, mind, and soul. He wants to free me from death itself. By letting his Firstborn die in my place. By allowing me to take the blood of the Lamb and smear it onto my doorframe so death may pass me by. That is what Jesus did for me and all of us. That is why God ordered to sacrifice a lamb every year after Israel left Egypt. To remind us and himself of the Firstborn that be slain to conquer death once and for all. So, after seeing my need for a saviour, reaching for me bound in my slavery, revealing to me the state I'm in, and breaking the spells of my idols, he sacrifices himself to break the curse of death over me. So I can step out of my mess and into his glory. The glory I was made for. That is how deep God's freedom runs. To death and back. And to eternity.

Just like the Children of Israel, Jesus' sacrifice brings me to a crossroads. If I want his death and resurrection to apply to me, if I want God to rescue me from eternal damnation, I have to actively step into his covenant. Have to say yes to follow his lead out of Egypt. Being raised by Christian parents I was always aware that God existed. I don't really have a conversion story. I never had this first, rousing encounter with God. He never needed to prove his existence to me. But I still had to make a choice. Missionary and Author, Ingrid Trobisch, used to say you cannot be a grandchild of God. So, just because my parents followed God, I wasn't automatically saved. I, too, am led to a crossroads by Jesus' offer of redemption. And must take the step into God's rescue plan myself. This step into God's covenant, this yes to his rescue plan is not a one-time thing. As I learn to walk with him I will again and again find myself at this crossroads. Again and again I find it to be my choice whether or not I want to follow God into his freedom. It is my step to take. And it is the greatest hope we have. To know that the death our sin bound us to is conquered and the path back to our Heavenly Father is open. Because God's Firstborn died for us, we can, whenever we find ourselves shackled by the consequences of our own self-determination, turn to God and ask for the blood of the Lamb. And again and again we will see Jesus' death and resurrection apply to us.

If you feel God whispering to your heart about the eternal life he wants to give you through the sacrifice of his Firstborn. If you feel him drawing you to himself, and inviting you to step into his covenant. If you, for the first or the hundredth time, realise that you need the Blood of the Lamb, the Death of the Firstborn, to save you from the death you deserved, you, too, are at a crossroads now. You can decide whether you are in or out. God will never force himself on you. All he does is offering you the mercy to let eternal death pass you by.

All you have to say is: "I'm in. I want to, maybe again, step into your covenant and follow your rescue plan. I want to become a part of Jesus' resurrection. I gladly accept your gift of redemption. Please come and change my life. Come and lead me into your perfect freedom. Teach me to look to you alone for security, provision, and fulfilment. I am all in."

As God has ordered them to millennia ago, his people remember and celebrate every year the moment when they first actively accepted his redemption by putting the lamb's blood onto their doorframes. Every year at Passover and every week at Shabbat. Christians of all denominations remember and celebrate the moment when they actively accepted God's deliverance by saying yes to his offer. Every Easter and every time they take communion. It is worthy to be celebrated. We need to remember. For it is the greatest mercy to be allowed into God's deep, everlasting freedom and back into his arms. Right were we belong.

If he had given us their wealth

In the same breath with the instructions for the Passover lamb and to be ready to leave Egypt for good, God also tells the Israelites to do something else. He sends them to go and ask their Egyptian neighbours for all kinds of articles of silver and gold. That must have been a strange order to obey. Why on earth would the Egyptians just give them anything, let alone gold and silver? It doesn't really make sense. But I guess, not much had made sense up until then, everything was still so shaken in the aftermath of the plagues. So maybe the Israelites just follow God's instructions because they don't know any better anymore. After all, the world is pretty much upside down at this point. So they go and ask the Egyptians for gold and silver and they find: God gives them favour with their oppressors. They give freely to the probably quite astonished Israelites.

That's a pretty unique way to plunder and pillage, isn't it? They just go to their oppressors and get all the treasures they ask for. Just like that. This is the first act of grace rather than mercy in God's rescue process. What do I mean by this distinction? Aren't mercy and grace synonyms? Not quite. Mercy is the goodness of not getting what we deserve and grace is the goodness of getting what we don't deserve. In his mercy, God takes his people out of slavery, frees them from the false gods they knew before him, and saves them from the death they deserved for their sins. Now in his grace he showers them with riches. And not just any riches, he showers them with the wealth of their oppressors.

I love that. Because that is what God's goodness towards me is like. Because of God's mercy I don't have to endure slavery, false hope, false security, lies, false gods, and death, even though I deserve it. And because of his grace it doesn't end there. God then showers me with goodness by giving life where there was death, comfort for despair, joy for sadness, health for sickness. And on top of that he turns my oppression into a victory by giving me authority over my past, and by turning that, which was supposed to destroy me, into a strength to glorify him.

I have seen God do this very same miracle everywhere. Marion was sexually abused by a family member in her childhood and had God comfort her, heal her wounds, restore her broken heart, and let her become a strong woman with healthy relationships and a loving family. And on top of that, she is constantly used by God to help others forgive, be healed, and set free from similar pasts. Her greatest pain was turned into a great victory by God's grace.

Anna suffered a miscarriage, openly mourned it, and shared her sadness, anger, and desperation with sometimes brutal honesty. She had women with the same experience coming out of the woodwork, who, because of Anna's open tears, finally realized that losing a baby was a bigger pain than they had allowed themselves to feel. Finally they dared to be honest and could embrace God's comfort and healing.

Carla experienced God's salvation and restoration after her burnout. Before, she had sought relaxation and strength in esoteric practices, which bound her spiritually and brought her panic attacks and insomnia. After God's deliverance she, guided by the Holy Spirit, turned her knowledge into a strategy to bring people out of their burnout into God's perfect freedom.

And I myself love to encourage people to finally let God take down the walls around their hearts, give up their self-protection, and ask him to be their protector instead, because I experienced how God freed me from my hardened heart myself. All treasures taken from the land of our oppression. All by the grace of God.

Because we live in a fallen world there is no guarantee we will never get hurt. But God grants us something even better: The treasures of the land of our oppression. That in all things God works for the good of those who love him. God's perfect liberation is also God's perfect victory. All we need to do is let him free us, comfort us, heal us, and then let him glorify himself by bringing forth the treasure of our own Egypt. And give us victory even though we did not deserve it.

If you feel battered and broken by your own personal Egypt, there is great hope for you. If you sometimes feel burdened by your past and like you still have to carry it, there is an amazing grace God wants to show you. He will give you the treasures of the land of your oppression. He will turn that, which was supposed to destroy you, into a victory for his glory. Maybe you can't see it yet. Maybe right now all you see is destruction and baggage. But God has promised, by the precedent he set with his people, that he will give you the treasures of your oppression. He will let all the things work for the good of those who love him. Whatever you entrust him with, the wounds, the pain, the failures, the devastation, he will turn to gold for his glory. All it takes is for you to allow him to free you. For you to put your past in his hands.

"God, I long to be freed from my past. I long for your comfort, your healing, and your life. In your mercy, rescue me, and in your grace, give me the treasures of my oppression."

It is his pleasure and our joy to see him turn our past into a golden future. And a grace beyond measure.

God's perfect deliverance

The first five stanzas of the Dayenu, the "Five Stanzas of Leaving Slavery", are, to me, the best exemplification of God's way to deliver. They perfectly reflect his process of breaking me free from oppression, sin, lies, and even death. I can use these five steps as a guideline and ask myself ever so often: Did God just find me shackled and oppressed by sin? Do I need to realise the severity of my own situation? Do I need to allow him to once more unmask what I have known so far as false idols? Do I need to remind myself again that God gave his Firstborn to save me from death? And do I trust him to turn my oppression into victory? No matter where I stand in that process, the next step will liberate me more and take me closer into the relationship I was created for. I love that. Deliverance could not be more perfect or more complete. And Israel is perfectly saved before they even respond to God's offer of love. That goes completely against our thinking. God doesn't even get anything out of it, yet. He has no guarantee Israel will even say yes to his covenant. This whole tremendous show of power might be in vain after all. And yet he does it. Because he wants to do everything and leave no stone unturned to offer us even the chance to answer his invitation. So that we might get to truly know him, might get closer to his heart, and might grasp the depth of his character and love for us. That we might see him as he truly is, was, and will be.

Maybe it's time to let him deliver you. Maybe it's time to acknowledge your need for a saviour. Maybe it's time to turn away from your false securities and your false sources of provision and fulfilment, and start to trust God to protect you, provide for you, and fulfil you. Maybe it's time to, for the first time or once again, take him up on his offer to deliver you from death. Maybe it's time to trust him with your past and let him turn your oppression into victory. Wherever you are right now, know that the next step will liberate you more and take you closer into the relationship you were created for.

For us, on our way to God's heart, this process is not a one-time thing. Sometimes we experience his perfect freedom in one area of our lives, while we keep God out of another area entirely. He will always walk where we are willing to follow him, and will always respect our no or not yet. And if you feel like you cannot trust God enough to follow him yet, he is patient and tender. He will never oppress or force you. It is okay to ask him to start over and show himself to you once more. Wherever you are right now, I wish you the tiny bit of faith it takes to say yes to the next step in God's rescue plan. Be it the first one or the twentieth. It will be the best one yet.

Provision Enough

The Five Stanzas of Miracles

I've heard so many preachers and Sunday school teachers talking reproachfully about the People of Israel and their constant complaining and persistent distrust in God. They have just seen God do amazing things and yet they still wish they'd have stayed in Egypt and say so at every little bump in the road. What on earth is their problem? If I had seen signs and wonders like this I would be running to God! Or would I? Beginning with the Dayenu-revelation, the more I thought about this and tried to imagine myself in their situation, the more I could understand their point of view.

Imagine living a slave life in ancient Egypt. Imagine the only gods you've ever seen being worshipped are of the silent kind. The kind you just thank for your good harvest and sacrifice some crops to, so they will keep making everything grow. You might have heard stories about a man called Abraham, who was said to have encountered God and whose grandson moved his family here during a famine, putting your whole people in this life of oppression. That's it. That is the extent your experiences with higher powers reach. Then along comes this guy Moses and says, the God of Abraham wants to come and save everyone. He performs a couple of miracles and you are amazed. Never ever have you seen any god actually do anything. This one does. Great. Everyone gets really excited. The hopes for finally leaving slavery get really high. Until this God starts to tear Egypt apart. Literally everything important gets destroyed and shaken up. Yes, Goshen is spared from the plagues, so apparently this God seems to be on your side. But how long will that last? How exhausting will it be to try and keep him from turning on you on a whim? Is that really the God we should follow into the desert? The guy, who just killed a child in every Egyptian family? That is the one we are going to trust to not let us starve in the desert if we don't worship him the way he likes? Congratulations to you, if you are relaxed and okay with it, I will stay worried, thank you very much.

Staying worried, maybe even a bit panicky, would be absolutely understandable, don't you agree? I think, at least some of the people went along on the trail out of Egypt because they were shocked into obedience rather than actually wanting to go. No wonder they can't bring themselves to trusting God yet. So he needs to make himself known some more. They have seen his omnipotence, seen him do everything to break them free from the clutches of slavery, false idols, and death, and lead them into victorious freedom. But they still don't really know him. They have yet to see his tender love, his caring heart. So far they have only seen him destroy and mercifully stop destroying. Now, in the desert, they finally get to see what he is willing to do to keep them alive, safe, and happy.

Again, he works in five steps, with five distinct revelations of his goodness and love. Each step, each miracle shows God as the provider. The provider of help, the provider of comfort, the provider of safety, the provider of food, even creating provision out of nothing. Like Israel, we need to see this side of God in our lives. To understand his love and the new dimension he led us into, we need this display of his goodness. If all we'd see is God wreaking havoc to break us free, we would be rightfully scared to follow him anywhere.

These five stanzas reveal that he is not just coming to break us free. He wants to be the source of all our provision. He wants to fill this hole in our souls, wants to take care of us by helping, comforting, saving, and feeding us. All the way through the sea, the desert, and into the Promised Land.

If he had split the sea for us

After centuries of slavery and a story of deliverance that shook an entire nation, Israel is finally free. They are finally allowed to leave. They head out of Egypt and into the desert towards Canaan, the Promised Land. But, because God knows the Children of Israel don't entirely trust him yet, he doesn't take them the direct route.

> *"When Pharaoh let the people go, God did not lead them on the road through the Philistine country, though that was shorter. For God said, 'If they face war, they might change their minds and return to Egypt.' So God led the people around by the desert road toward the Red Sea." (Exodus 13:17+18)*

Imagine the elation, the joy, the excitement: They are really leaving slavery behind! How wonderful! God himself, appearing as a pillar of cloud by day and a pillar of fire by night, goes before them, leading his people out of oppression. But where is he leading them? This road seems to head towards the sea, why are we going there? Imagine the confusion and frustration amongst Israel when they realise: this pillar of cloud guides them to a dead end. And then the rising panic when suddenly the mysterious pillar in front of them is not the only cloud anymore, because behind them, stomping up the desert sand, the Egyptian chariots are in hot pursuit. Their oppressors obviously changed their minds about letting them go and instead have become unrelenting persecutors. Israel is caught in a trap. Before them the sea, behind them the Egyptian hosts. Is this what God had in mind when staging his great rescue operation? To have them now either drowned or massacred?

"As Pharaoh approached, the Israelites looked up, and there were the Egyptians, marching after them. They were terrified and cried out to the Lord. They said to Moses, 'Was it because there were no graves in Egypt that you brought us to the desert to die? What have you done to us by bringing us out of Egypt? Didn't we say to you in Egypt, 'Leave us alone; let us serve the Egyptians'? It would have been better for us to serve the Egyptians than to die in the desert!'" (Exodus 14:10-12)

I can't blame them. It doesn't make sense. It seems so arbitrary. How did they even end up in this situation? Is God just making things up as he goes or did he bring them here on purpose? Couldn't he have taken them a safer route, maybe a road that leads somewhere around the sea, past the Philistines, and far away from the Egyptian hosts? He is God after all. He should know what he is doing, right? He does. Again, he told Moses so beforehand.

"Then the Lord said to Moses: Tell the Israelites to turn back and encamp near Pi Hahiroth, between Migdol and the sea. They are to encamp by the sea, directly opposite Baal Zephon. Pharaoh will think, 'The Israelites are wandering around the land in confusion, hemmed in by the desert.' And I will harden Pharaoh's heart, and he will pursue them. But I will gain glory for myself through Pharaoh and all his army, and the Egyptians will know that I am the I AM." (Exodus 14:1-4)

There it is. God actually brought Israel to the sea on purpose. Not just to avoid the Philistines, but to, again, glorify himself as the God who comes to his people's rescue. He wants them to know he will make a way for them. Even in the most terrifying circumstances he will provide help and guidance. He knows they need to see this side of him. They need to meet the way maker, the God who will split the sea for the people he loves. Who will never be overwhelmed by circumstances and will always break through and bring life were there seemed to be only death. And to be able to reveal himself as a way maker, he needs to lead his people into a situation with no way out. Even if that means enduring their wailing and accusing.

Only one Israelite is undeterred by the predicament they are in: Moses. The one man who didn't grow up under the oppression of slavery. Who didn't grow up under the threat of being completely at the mercy of Pharaoh's capricious moods. And, most importantly, the only man who had encountered God face to face before. Encountering God is always a fundamental experience. It tends to ground and steady you, tends to give you the confidence to trust and follow him. So when the people cry out to him, Moses doesn't waver nor despair, but answers them:

"Do not be afraid. Stand firm and you will see the deliverance the Lord will bring you today." (Exodus 14:13)

And they do. Boy, do they ever. God makes a way for them. A unique, amazing, slightly terrifying way. He tells Moses to raise his staff and bring it down on the water. The seas part, two walls of water rise, leaving a miraculous but scary pathway to the other side. God reveals himself as the way maker and he himself, the cloud of his presence, keeps the Egyptian hosts at bay while Israel starts walking through the Red Sea.

Just like he did with Israel, God often leads us into situations with no way out. Sometimes by simply letting us realise the severity of our circumstances. Sometimes by letting life in a fallen world run its course. Sometimes by lovingly leading us to a dead end where the oppressors of our own past seem to persecute us while there is still no way towards a bright new future before us. He does this because he wants to reveal himself as the one who helps and saves. As the one who will drain the seas to keep his promise to us. As the one who will never forsake us. Who will always come for us, always save us, always make a way for us. Who is for us no matter what. And who watches our backs the entire time we walk down the way he made for us.

Like Israel we tend to worry and wish we were back in our own personal Egypt where we at least knew our way around. Like Israel we feel trapped and don't understand why and how we ended up in a situation with no way out. Sometimes we even blame God the way Israel did. Like Israel we have the opportunity to hear: "Do not be afraid. Stand firm and you will see the deliverance the Lord will bring you today." And like Israel we will encounter God as the one who will drain the seas to come for us, save us, and make a way.

My brother Tobias had had a very exhausting, stressful year already when the news of my father's imminent death reached him. Only two months before he had handed in his dissertation and was preparing for the defence of his doctor's thesis, scheduled for Friday. While on Wednesday our other siblings and me made arrangements to travel to hopefully see our father one last time, Tobias couldn't even let himself think about that for fear of losing focus. Dad died in the early hours of Thursday, my brother got his doctor's degree on Friday and joined us at my parent's house around midnight. On Sunday, my siblings drove back home again because of work and family obligations, only my brother-in-law and I could stay and help our Mom.

Naturally, our family group chat was very busy with all the coordination and information needed to organise a funeral. But on Monday, between all the casket styles and flower arrangements and whatnot, my brother simply posted: "Just so you know, it still can get wilder, I was just terminated for operational reasons. Prayer is welcome." To his wife he said that night: "This was one thing too many." They were both emotionally paralysed, couldn't even find words to tell God how they felt. All they could muster was a desperate: "You need to do something now, we have no strength and no faith left."

Out of despair rather than trust they stood still and waited for the deliverance the Lord would bring them. And he did. On Wednesday, only two days after the news of his termination, a friend of his offered Tobias a job, because God had put it on his heart to do so. Same pay, fewer hours, better work environment. God had come through for them and made a way where there hadn't been any prospects. Tobias and his family encountered God as their saviour, way maker, and provider that day. And that encounter strengthened their faith, so when a few months later their car broke down with no money to buy a new one, they didn't just stand still but stood firm, awaiting the deliverance of the Lord. And again, he came through for them.

Lauren was working hard to develop a highly efficient program to help people with burnout syndrome when she and her team reached a point where progress seemed to stop and be stuck in one stage of development. They had already achieved a lot, the building blocks for the program were finished and ready to be tested. But somehow there was no interest in the product. Nobody came to receive the help and guidance the program could give. Frustrated with the stagnation, Lauren and I prayed. For a breakthrough, for a word from God, for just something we could do to move the program along. The Holy Spirit answered with a vision. I saw Lauren's spa hotel being cut off from the outside world by a road under heavy construction. So we started praying for God to finish the construction, open up the road, and make a way for the product to reach the customers and for the guests to reach the hotel. His response was to reveal himself as the saviour, the way maker, and the provider. Not only did he send people Lauren's way who helped with the marketing, but interested guests started coming, and the further development and polishing of the program could continue. Also, God quite literally opened up the road towards the hotel: a motorway feeder road, connecting the state road to the hotel with the nearest motor way, got finally finished, and someone in management had been moved to put the name of our town on the motorway exit sign, bringing more recognition to the town.

Hillary was studying for her midterm exams to become a special needs teacher when the pressure got too much for her. Not only the upcoming test stressed her but also all the hopes and dreams her mother had for her. Truth be told, Hillary hadn't chosen this profession herself. Rather, it had been her mother's unfulfilled dream to teach special needs kids, so she had put everything into having her daughter go where she herself couldn't. Hillary had failed the exams once before and now was her last chance to pass them. If she failed again, her mother's heart would be broken, and she herself would never be allowed to teach special needs again. The pressure grew with the exams drawing nearer and the evening before the test Hillary prayed to God in desperation. She asked him to make a way for her, to help her through all this. And he did.

Immediately a calming peace came over Hillary, it lasted through her last learning session, all through the night, and all the way through the exams. She had peace and felt held and protected by God. And she failed the test miserably. Some save, you might say. But, oh, it was. God saved Hillary that day. Saved her from a career she'd never wanted and that would have destroyed her. Saved her from her mother's relentless controlling of her life. And saved her mother from losing face in front of her friends, because she could now simply blame the exams committee for her daughter's failing and subsequent career change, and portray Hillary as the brave young lady, who found a different path, now that her heart's desire had been taken from her. By letting her fail peacefully, God made a way for Hillary to actually study what she wanted and have a life after her own heart, all while growing closer and closer to the one who loved and saved her.

I am sure you experienced dead ends in your life before. And maybe you wondered how you got into a situation with no way out. Maybe you even find yourself stuck between a rock and a hard place right now. Maybe you asked yourself whether you missed a turn or misread the signs to seemingly end up so far from God's path for you. Maybe you already despaired, blamed God for all this, and wished yourself back to your personal Egypt for the comfort of familiarity. Or maybe you started praying against the attack you feel yourself being under. All these are valid reactions to a double bind. But I want to encourage you to start looking for God's purpose behind these situations and maybe ask a new question: "God, what do you want me to know about you? How will you make yourself known to me this time?"

Because even if he didn't turn all the circumstances against you himself, he just loves to reveal himself to you like you've never seen him before. He will take any chance he can get. And his revelation will always lead you to a new level of knowing him, a new level of freedom, and a new level of fulfilment.

I have seen God be my way maker time and time again and can tell you, just like Moses: "Do not be afraid. Stand firm and you will see the deliverance the Lord will bring you today." He WILL come through, he WILL make a way, even if it means draining the seas for you, and he WILL have your back through it all. So stand firm and just ask him: "God, I don't see a way out of this. I need you to make one. I long to get to know you as the saviour, the way maker, and the provider. Please reveal yourself to me as my saviour once more. Please make a way through this and please have my back while I follow your path. Thank you for never forsaking me and being for me, all the way out of slavery, through the sea, and into the Promised Land."

I wish you the courage and the trust in God to, from now on, view every predicament you find yourself in as a great opportunity to encounter a side of God you haven't seen before. I know it will strengthen your faith and will increasingly become easier to do. Every time you see God come to your rescue and miraculously make a way for you, will cement your trust in him more than before. And bit by bit he will establish himself in your heart as the one true saviour, way maker, and provider. The one worthy of all your trust, all your heart, and all your life.

If he had taken us through the sea on dry land

After turning to him in his desperation, God tells Moses:

"Raise your staff and stretch out your hand over the sea to divide the water so that the Israelites can go through the sea on dry ground." (Exodus 14:16)

Moses does so and immediately a strong eastern wind arises and blows the waters apart. What a sight it must have been! The seas splitting before their eyes, rising into two gigantic walls of water, defying the laws of physics left and right, and in-between a path to the other side. It is just what they needed, but it also is illogical, awe-inspiring, miraculous, and utterly terrifying. Who would want to walk through there? The Hebrews sure don't. Their knees must have been shaking. But behind them, the Egyptian hosts are held back by the godly cloud pillar, and it is quite obvious they haven't given up and are still trying to get to the people of Israel. So maybe the threat of the chariots helps to move people along a bit. They actually start walking towards the marvellous road and there they find something astonishing. The path is dry and surprisingly easy to walk on. You would expect quite a slippery affair, climbing over rocks and navigating through mud, with the occasional unlucky fish flopping about or something like that. But no, to everyone's amazement, the road is completely dry and easily manageable for the old and the young alike. It is a miracle in itself. A miracle of grace rather than mercy. God, in his mercy, reveals himself as the saviour and way maker, and then, in his grace, he sees to it that the way he makes is marvellously easy to walk.

We can see this principle in other stories in the bible as well. The breakthroughs God gives always open ways that are fairly easy to walk. When God gave Goliath into David's hands he also miraculously opened a way for Israel to defeat the Philistine army. All they had to do was chase after them while the Philistines fled, although this army was bigger and better equipped and would have had a very good chance of victory over Israel, even without Goliath. When Gideon, living oppressed by Midian, was visited by the angel of God and given the grace to defeat the armies of the Midianites and the Amalekites, his soldiers don't even need to fight. Instead they can watch their enemies slaughter each other in their fear.

That is something we, too, can look forward to: For the road made for us to be easy to walk on. Whenever we find ourselves in a situation where we need a miracle to get out, God is not only showing mercy when we turn to him in desperation, but grace by providing a smooth road. My brother Tobias' job offer was not only miraculously perfectly timed, it was better than the job he had lost. For the same salary plus a month's pay as a Christmas bonus it gave him more family time, right when he needed it the most. At his old job he oftentimes had found himself having to mediate between his boss and his colleague, and generally working under a lot of pressure due to interpersonal tension in the company. His new job, on the other hand, had him working with a well-established team in an appreciative work environment. In his mercy, God had made a way where there hadn't been one, and in his grace, the path was easy to walk.

Lauren and I had prayed for a breakthrough in the process of development. And God, in his mercy, answered and provided not only new connections and new guests but, in his grace, also literally a road easier to travel.

Hillary experienced God's mercy and peace as an answer to her prayer. And then in his grace, he let her fail her exam and brought her freedom and new life she would never had dared asking for. It changed her career, her relationship with her mother, her relationship with God, basically her entire life. She did not just have peace but could breathe again and grow to become the woman God made her to be.

So if you find yourself in need for God's mercy to make a way where there isn't one right now, but also in fear of that way being too challenging, take heart. The road God makes for you when you need his breakthrough will be just as dry and easy to walk as the Red Sea was for Israel. Maybe your knees are shaking at the prospect of following God down a road he just opened up for you. Maybe you feel like you are being forced to follow it by your pursuing oppressors rather than being drawn by God. Maybe everything in you is sounding the alarm to beware and not throw yourself into this path that is defying the laws of physics. It is completely understandable and no disgrace whatsoever to be cautious. But know one thing: God's freedom is perfect. In his mercy he will provide a way, and in his grace it will be dry and easy to manage for the old and the young alike. Because he loves you. And when he reveals himself as your saviour and way maker, you will know him as your provider and fulfilment as well.

So just dare to take the first step. The road will be surprisingly easy to walk. Just say: "Father, I am scared and fear I might not trust you enough. But I am amazed at your mercy making a way for me. I also want to trust the promise of your grace that the road will be dry and easy to walk. Thank you for loving me so much. Thank you for once more taking me to a new level in our relationship."

I promise you, this new level will be good for you. It will fill you with life, and strengthen your faith in him. And it will be the best one yet.

If he had drowned our oppressors in the sea

The road through the Red Sea must have been a marvellous thing to behold, not only for Israel but for the Egyptians as well. No one had ever seen such a sight before, so I bet Pharaoh and his hosts were in awe. Not for long though, because as soon as the pillar of cloud lifts away from them, all 600 Egyptian chariots thunder after Israel, again in hot pursuit. This seems excessively mad to me. Why on earth would they trust this unnatural path enough to drive between two physics-defying walls of water? While Israel was forced through there by their oncoming oppressors, Egypt could have easily just turned away from this watery death-trap and gone home. But no, they continue their chase. And as soon as horse and chariot enter the path between water they, again, face the God of Israel, fighting for his people. He jams their wheels and they all get stuck in the mud. Mud, mind you, that hadn't been there when the Children of Israel walked through there on dry land just moments ago. Only now the Egyptians start to fear what they are up against.

> *"Let's get away from the Israelites! The Lord is fighting for them against Egypt." (Exodus 14:25)*

So they turn and try to run, but too late. God tells Moses to stretch out his hand over the sea, and the waters rush back and close over Pharaoh and his hosts. 600 chariots, their horses and drivers, drowned.

Again, you would think there could have been an easier way. Why would the pillar of cloud not just keep the Egyptian armies at bay, until Israel had safely crossed the sea and the waters had closed up again? God's people would have been safe from the hosts anyway, separated by the sea. Why again such destruction? Also, why did Pharaoh chase after Israel at all? Weren't the Egyptians devastated by the death of their firstborn and all the havoc God had wreaked in their land? Didn't they have enough? Why would they pursue Israel after God had shown with such might, what he was willing to do to save his people?

God made them. He, again, hardened the heart of Pharaoh, and made the Egyptians follow Israel. He held them off long enough for his people to cross the sea, and then made them blindly chase after them into the parted sea, driving right into their watery demise. He let their wheels get stuck and then had the waters close over them. And again, he told Moses so beforehand, also giving his reason.

"Pharaoh will think, 'The Israelites are wandering around the land in confusion, hemmed in by the desert.' And I will harden Pharaoh's heart, and he will pursue them. But I will gain glory for myself through Pharaoh and all his army, and the Egyptians will know that I am the I AM." (Exodus 14:3-4)

Drowning their oppressors is part of God's plan to reveal himself to Israel as their saviour. For his rescue is not just about escape. It is about salvation. Not just running away from oppression but seeing it destroyed. Seeing every effect it had on them eliminated. God wants Israel and us to know him as the one who fights for his people. If we follow him, we won't have to be on the run. We won't have to worry our past might catch up with us again. He will not only remove me from my oppressors, but eradicate them entirely if I ask him. So they can never come after me again. He will not have me struggle forever, his freedom is perfect. And HE is the one doing the fighting. While I just follow the path he opened up, he clears my persecutors out behind me.

Susanne worked as an emergency room nurse and therefore saw things on a daily basis, that weren't always easy to stomach. So, like most of her colleagues, she would smoke cigarettes to calm her nerves. A lot of them. Every break she got. So when she gave her life to Jesus, she was a passionate chain-smoker. That day she experienced God's perfect deliverance. He not only took her life into his loving hands, he also took her longing for cigarettes away from her. She immediately stopped craving them, and when she, more out of habit than desire, lit one, she got sick to her stomach. Perfect freedom. While Susanne followed God's path, he destroyed her oppressors behind her, freeing her from her destructive cravings completely.

Michael used almost any kind of drug hoping to cope with the memories of his childhood in foster homes and on the streets. Just anything to fill the hole in his soul and drown out the feelings of inadequacy and rejection. Until he met God in a life-changing encounter. Being embraced and comforted by his heavenly father, receiving healing and love, guidance and purpose all at once freed Michael from addiction immediately. He walked the newly opened path into God's love and complete acceptance while behind him God cleared away his oppressors.

I've heard stories just like Susanne's and Michael's from people talking about all kinds of addictions and psychological problems. Alcohol, drugs, esoteric practices, anxiety attacks, depression, you name it. God doesn't work the same way with everyone and everything, but his freedom is always perfect.

On my own path with God I have seen this same miracle in a more subtle way. I was taking courses to study and learn to be a counsellor for burned-out and grieving people at the time. I had been part of a team developing a program to conquer and resolve burnout and it became necessary for some of us to become coaching counsellors in that program. But because I had no experience with burnout myself, I was worried I might not be much help to my clients. I felt, I was at an impasse. So I asked God to come to my rescue and he did. Step by step, coaching session by coaching session, he taught me to stay in constant contact with the Holy Spirit, just saying and doing what he prompted me to say and do. Therefore HE worked in the lives of the clients, bringing them deliverance, provision, and fulfilment. I was just a first-hand spectator. It was counselling entirely surrendered to God. And therefore entirely free from manipulation.

After my own experiences with manipulative counsellors, who meant well and thought they knew better, I had been afraid of maybe turning into one as well, because it was the counselling I was used to. In general it comes very easy to me to see people's true hearts, fears, and meaning behind the things they are willing to tell. So it also comes easy to give well-meant, sometimes even good counsel to them. But that is not the same as giving God, even if my advice is sometimes wise and useful. So while I needed to surrender my wisdom and myself to God to be able to give God to my burnout clients, I grew accustomed to merely being a vessel for the Holy Spirit. Now, I work like that, no matter what the client's issue is. Because I learned: even my best advice and ideas are nothing compared to what God wants to give to the client. After all, while I can only guess or assume what the client needs, God KNOWS. While I can only be kind and helpful to the client, God longs to deliver, protect, and fulfil them with strength and love.

Now, I smell manipulation from a mile away and made it a habit to ask the Holy Spirit to purify my heart time and time again, so that whatever manipulation is in me gets eradicated like the Egyptian hosts.

What God does by drowning our oppressors behind us, Paul describes like this:

> *"Therefore, if anyone is in Christ, the new creation has come: The old has gone, the new is here!" (2. Corinthians 5:17)*

If we put ourselves in God's hands and follow his path, we become a new creation, freed from our past. We do not just escape but are made untouchable. That is his promise and our hope. So whenever we struggle with our past catching up with us, whenever we feel our oppressors chasing us down, God wants to not only make a way to escape. He wants to eradicate our pursuers and bring us complete freedom, while we just follow his path. And we can hold him to it.

Maybe you don't feel like a new creation. Maybe you know, deep down, you are the same poor wretch who needed God to save them from oppression. Maybe you feel your victory over your past is barely noteworthy. Maybe you even feel ashamed about your continuing need for rescue. No matter what you fear or what your circumstances might tell you, God's miraculous rescue and eradication of your oppressors are close at hand. You just ask him.

"Father, thank you for laying this marvellous path, over dry land and into your freedom, at my feet. Thank you for helping me walk it. I put my past and my oppressors into your hands. Please eradicate them and make me untouchable for them. Thank you for fighting for me. Thank you for making me this new creation."

Just like my struggle to be free from manipulative behaviour this might be a question of holding on to God and sometimes reminding your soul that you are, in fact, a new creation. I have seen God sometimes let me experience situations similar to past struggles, which can feel like old temptation creeping up again. But he doesn't do that to test me. He does it to show me where I am now compared to where I used to be. And believe me, these brushes with temptation will be easier to conquer than you imagine right now. They will continue to get easier. Remember: God's perfect deliverance involves him taking matters into his mighty hands, eradicating your oppressors, and bringing you into his fullness. It is his fight, not yours. Let him fight it. Just enjoy being the beneficiary of his victory.

If he had supplied for our needs in the desert for 40 years

They really don't get much time to breathe. After watching the Egyptian society crumble around them under God's judgement, being chased down by Pharaoh's hosts, seeing the seas split before them, and their oppressors drowned behind them, God's people are stranded in the desert. No wonder they are a little shaken. They are free, but far from wealthy. The land they left for this was fruitful and they are not used to being hungry. Until now. Now they left all of the riches of Egypt behind. So, naturally they look for water and food. And whenever they cannot find anything, they use the same technique to survive that kept them alive as slaves in Egypt: They wail and scream about abuse and starvation. As slaves who would lose in value if mistreated, that is the way to get slave drivers to behave less cruel. So that is the way Israel addresses God. Not by asking for help, not by turning to him as the source of all good things, but by accusing him of planning to kill them, until Moses steps in and prays to God for intervention. And despite the distrust his people throw at him, he answers by revealing his love for them. He knows where this distrust comes from. He knows: Rather than a problem of rebellion or lack of understanding, it is a problem of a slave's mindset. Because slaves is what they still are.

Being born and raised in slavery, their health and strength defines their worth. And this always has been their only bargaining chip. Screaming about hunger, thirst, or dying was the only way to draw attention to misconduct of cruel slave drivers. After all, mistreating and starving slaves meant devaluing property. Israel knew their worth in Egypt. They knew, they were as valuable as the work they could do, so their lives and wellbeing were cared for. Yes, they had to work hard, but if they did, the Egyptians kept them alive and healthy. So, of course, Israel idealised the land of their oppression. Of course they remembered fondly the steady, dependable provision and dreary but mostly reliable life in Egypt, conveniently forgetting their desperation before. Of course they deeply mistrust this God, who has come along, saying he loved and wanted to free them, because they can't grasp what he wants them for. So they don't know where they stand with him, they don't know the value they have in his eyes and how immeasurable it is compared to their worth in Egypt. They cannot believe he just wants to love them and provide for them, without demanding any work in return. They cannot believe he wants them as children and friends, and not as servants. Even though God has already started to show them what it means to live under his grace and directly out of his hand. Depending on him reminds them of slavery and his perfect freedom doesn't feel like they are their own masters. Again, they confuse freedom with self-determination and depending on God alone with oppression, just like Adam and Eve before them.

God wants his people to be truly free. Not only from their oppressors but from the mindset of a slave. Free to live under his grace, free to believe the value he has given them, free to trust in his goodness, free to know they don't need a bargaining chip with him, free to grasp that he just loves them because he is love, not because they earned it. So he puts them all in a situation where he is the only source of security, provision, and fulfilment. A situation where they can't do anything but live by grace and let him love them.

It is so important to him that his people know him as the God who loves them, that he would rather stay in the desert with them for forty years, keeping them alive day by day, than have them settle in the Promised Land without truly knowing him. So, when after the first two years of seeing God provide for them, fight for them, and love them, they still don't trust him to give them Canaan as a home or victory over its inhabitants, this is where he stays with them: in the desert. To reveal himself and his love to them. To deeply establish the value they have in his eyes in their hearts. Because he sees them still struggling under the curse of a slave's mindset and the fear of being at the mercy of an unknown God, he keeps them close to himself.

The desert is a place of death for Israel. It is a place where they are stripped of everything they relied on. It is a place for their slave's mindset to die. But it is also a place of resurrection. A place where the people of Israel finally learn what value they have in God's eyes, how he protects them, how he provides for them, and how he loves them.

Here in the wilderness they experience a time where they literally live from hand to mouth. Miracle to miracle, God reveals himself as the loving provider. The first water source they reach is bitter, so God tells Moses to throw in a certain piece of bark and the water immediately turns sweet and drinkable. At other times God lets water spring from rocks. He lets bread and fowl rain from heaven. He gives them victory over any enemies they come across. And he keeps them strong and in good health all the way. For 40 years Israel sees God as the provider of security and life. They learn that nourishment and sustenance come from him. He takes care of them, answers every possible need. He reveals himself as the giver of every good thing, and he is not bound by any special location, he is the source of all life after all.

It is such a precious, important, life-altering revelation: God is the loving provider and true source of every good thing. The moment his people understand, the moment I as his child understand that God is good, wants to shower us with love, and answer any need we might have, that moment changes everything. That is why God takes 40 years to really make sure Israel gets to know this side of him and let this truth sink in. It is actually so important to God, he decrees his people to remember it, not only every spring celebrating Passover, but also every fall celebrating Sukkot, the Feast of the Tabernacles. For this festival Jews around the world live in huts, commemorating their time in the desert, where they were completely dependent on God alone. Showing they trust him alone, look to him alone, seek his help alone, his love alone, his provision alone. Because they know, believe, and trust he is the true source for every good thing, the first place to go to with whatever they may need.

To this day God longs to be known as the loving provider. He longs for us to know him as the true source of every good thing, as the answer to every need, as the first place to go to with whatever we may lack or want. And to this day he reveals himself miracle by miracle. I have heard and seen so many stories of God showering people with his love, providing every good thing.

The night before I was supposed to take the theoretical exam for my driving test, for which I admittedly hadn't studied enough, I put the test and myself into God's hands. I told him, I needed to go to bed now and was completely dependent on him regarding that exam. If he wanted me to pass the test, I would be happy, but I would totally understand, if he wanted to teach me to study more by letting me fail now. I got up an hour early the next morning.

In front of me lay a stack of training questionnaires, the Holy Spirit gave me the page numbers of three of them, and I worked them over. I felt very guided by God already, but he kept on showering me with signs of love. On the way to my driving school he gave me the most beautiful sunrise to look at. Then I was picked up at the school and driven to the exam in my favourite car, a silver 1997 Mercedes ML. And when I was handed my exam questionnaire the first question was the same as on one of the training questionnaires I had studied two hours earlier, so this time I knew the correct answer. God let me pass my test and on the way there showed his love for me again and again.

John was planning to make his hotel more energy efficient and was having trouble finding a good contractor with the right concept for the building. He met with several companies but none of the offers were as well of a fit as John had hoped. The project had already dragged on for weeks and was occupying most of his thoughts, making him worry, and starting to affect his sleep. One day, his wife had enough. "Let's put this into God's hands. We need a miracle from him. And we want this to be his hotel, anyway, so he should be the one bringing in a contractor after his own heart." And that he did. Less than a week later Charles, one of the regular guests, approached John with a proposition: "I heard you need an energy efficient heating system. My company are leading experts in that field. I would like to help you find and install the perfect solution for your house. I will work free of charge and find you the best materials and workers. This hotel has been a home away from home for me and my wife for years, I would love to give something back."

Charles was not only serious, he was also not overselling himself or his company. They installed a co-generator unit which not only drastically reduced the hotel's power consumption, it enabled them to feed energy back into the local supply network. Now, whenever Charles and his wife stay at the hotel, he regularly does the maintenance for the system, still free of charge. What a blessing God sent to answer John's prayer!

In 2007 Monica's hotel was partly under construction. The new outdoor pool took a bit longer than expected, and because of this the guests stopped coming. The numbers dropped dramatically and money started to get tight. So Monica and her husband prayed for a miracle of provision. The very next day the phones started to ring again. It was like God had awakened fond memories of the hotel in people so they changed their vacation plans and stopped by. Two days later the construction workers' union called to strike and even dropped by Monica's pool to force the workers to stop working. Another worrisome development, another reason to fear money loss. So Monica prayed again, and God provided again. It only took a smile and a tray of drinks to make the union guys leave peacefully, because God gave Monica favour with them. And, thank God, construction could proceed.

Knowing and working with Monica actually had a great impact on me and my journey to know God as my provider. When I met her, her life with God had only just begun and, being a very positive and very literal person, she had an enviably child-like faith. It was the most natural thing in the world for her to take God up on his word. "Well, if it is written here, that we are to see and do greater things than Jesus' disciples, we just have to go and ask God for them, don't we?" she said, pointing to the Bible. So we did just that. No matter what came up, no matter which need we had, Monica would always say: "We need to pray again. We need God here." And God always answered. Always. And quite quickly as well. The more we experienced God's fast provision, the easier it was to ask him. Now, it goes without saying for both Monica and me that God will provide whatever we may need.

Sandra and her family were about to set out from Florida on a cruise in the Gulf of Mexico, when there were unexpected complications with the booking. It seemed like they would not be able to go on the trip after all. Only a week before, Sandra had asked God to reveal to her the meaning of the verse

He provides for those he loves even while they sleep. (Psalm 127:2b)

And now she reminded God of that and asked him to help with the holiday. She went to bed and when she got up the next morning, she found everything settled for the family cruise. The German travel agency had worked all morning, while Sandra in Florida was still sleeping, to organise everything. God literally provided for the ones he loves while they slept.

Just like God is still revealing himself as the loving provider of all good things, he also still sometimes keeps us in the desert to make sure to free us from our slave's mindset. This process of changing our minds can be quite exhausting and can go quite deep. Depending on how far the roots of our slavery and oppression go. To grasp what God tries to do in the desert, the image in my head is that of trees. Let me elaborate. For over a decade I lived in the Harz, a highland area in the northern middle of Germany. It's a very rainy and therefore very green region, with mixed forest and moss-covered craggy cliffs and boulders dominating the landscape. One fascinating aspect accompanying the frequent rain is that some trees, especially birches, manage to grow right in the cracks of the rocks. They cling on to steep cliffs with their roots, bending 90 degrees to then grow upwards towards the sun. It almost looks like they are trying to climb up to reach higher ground. Inspiring, how little nature needs to get by. Compared to the strong, old trees growing by the little streams flowing at the foot of those cliffs, though, these climbing birches are way less equipped to survive serious storms, heatwaves, and droughts. These two types of very different looking trees always remind me of that verse in Jeremiah:

"Blessed is the one who trusts in the Lord, whose confidence is in him. They will be like a tree planted by the water that sends out its roots by the stream. It does not fear when heat comes; its leaves are always green. It has no worries in a year of drought and never fails to bear fruit." (Jeremiah 17:7-8)

These trees are the image in my mind whenever I put something into God's hands. Because when he inevitably comes for me and lets all things work for my good, it feels like he plucks me off the cliff I had been clinging to and plants me firmly by the water instead. He exchanges the little rain I managed with for a constant, flowing stream of provision, lets me straighten up, lets me send out my roots, and has me growing strong.

In my process toward learning to let God protect my heart rather than hardening it to hopefully remain unscathed by the world, God led me through three consecutive times in the desert. One after the other my three closest friends ended our respective friendships, seemingly because they rather wanted to live a life without God, especially without his guidelines regarding purity, and wanted to avoid my judgement. Back then I was convinced they just couldn't stand Jesus in me, because he made their conscience scream so loud and made their lives in sin feel so shameful. Now I know that the judge in me was by far the more unbearable part. But I needed to judge them, because that shielded my heart from the pain it caused me to see them stray and to have them drop me as a friend. And it took me three times in the desert to finally let go of that craggy cliff I was clinging to. The first two times I at some point decided to stop crying and stop caring. Which only worked by – you probably guessed it already – hardening my heart. The third time I finally let God pluck me off that rock and plant me by the water. I had realised the repeated pattern and became so desperate at the thought of maybe having to experience this for a fourth time that I told God: "Dad, I want to learn everything you want to teach me with this right now! I don't want to go another round. I surrender! I will cry until you come and comfort me. I will not take up my old weapons and defend myself. I will let this open wound bleed until you heal me. I want to see you lead me through this. I won't take shortcuts, I won't decide for myself whether enough is enough. Only you are enough." Finally I put my trust in God to be my provider. Finally I let go of that craggy cliff, put my heart, my pain, my sense of justice, my longing for retribution, and my hope for vindication into his hands.

It was a breakthrough. Not only did I finally learn to be protected by God, I learned the difference between being truly comforted and simply stopping to cry. I learned the difference between discerning right from wrong and judging people. And I learned to ask God for mercy and grace for the people around me whenever the judge in me started to rear its ugly head again. I never want to go back to those old habits, it is truly good riddance. Being comforted, healed, and protected by God is so immeasurably better, easier, and deeper than any defence I could manage on my own.

God is still the I Am, the same yesterday, today, and tomorrow. So just like Israel before us (and still) we can ask for provision in any circumstance. He loves us so much, he opens wells for us, gives us victory in our battles, and life where circumstances promised death. Like children, trusting in his goodness, we may ask and he will provide. If we, who are evil, give our children what they need, how much more will our father in heaven, who is perfect, provide for us (Matthew 7:11)? He wants to be known as the source of all good things, all blessings, all life on earth. He has everything we could ever need at his disposal and in abundance. He longs to shower us with all his love and grace. So that we may know him as our provider and ourselves as his beloved children, not his servants. There is no need to wail and scream about abuse and starvation like slaves addressing a cruel slave driver. There is no need to prove ourselves worthy of a little bit of mercy. God wants us to know ALL his grace. If we start seeing him as the only true source of all provision and life, the thought of being dependent on him will become more and more appealing. And like Israel every year we, too, can start celebrating his grace and goodness. We, too, can show we trust him alone, look for him alone, seek his help alone, his love alone, his provision alone. And have him be the first place to go to with whatever we may need.

Maybe you're not there yet. Maybe you still feel like you need to struggle to deserve his grace, or even pay off his mercy first. Maybe you have yet to see God working miracles like this in your life. Maybe you can't wrap your head around the thought of having a loving father who wants to be the source for every good thing. Or maybe, like Israel, you have seen God do great things for you, provide for you, and give you victory, yet somehow he still isn't your first place to go to with whatever you may need. Wherever you stand right know, know that God is the source of every good thing and all life. Know that he is neither bound by location nor the laws of nature to answer your need. Know that he loves you and longs to shower you with abundant blessings. Let the Holy Spirit use your time in the desert to drive this precious, life-altering revelation into your heart. It is a game changer. Again, all you have to do is ask.

"Heavenly Father, I want to know you as my provider and myself as your beloved child. Please free me from my slave's mindset and let me truly understand the value you give me. Please forgive my distrust and change my heart. I want to trust you alone, look to you alone, seek your help alone, your love alone, your provision alone. I want to know, believe, and trust you are the true source for every good thing. I want to let go of that craggy cliff and have you plant me by the waters. Holy Spirit, please teach me to look for God as my first place to go to with whatever I may need."

Let the game change. Let God change your mindset. Let him be your source of all provision and life. Let him shower you with abundant grace. Look to him in everything. If you put everything into God's hands, you will start to see God's hand in everything. It might be a leap of faith. It might feel challenging or even scary. But I promise you, things will never be the same again.

If he had fed us manna

Of all the blessings and provision God showers his people with, one is standing out. He does far more than just bringing forth what nature has to offer. He literally lets bread rain from heaven. After Israel cried out to him for food he sends something sweet and nourishing with the morning dew. What is it?, they ask. Manna? What is it God is creating out of thin air? What is it that is just appearing in the morning and rotting overnight, but not on the Shabbat? It is constant, never changing, and unending. It is keeping them alive, fed, and healthy until they reach the Promised Land. No matter how much or how little they gather in the mornings, everyone always has enough. It is a perfect system of basic supply for everyone, a basic income guarantee. And it never fails, not once in forty years. Neither rebellion nor mutiny, neither Golden Calves nor uprisings against Moses change anything about this constant provision.

It is just what they need in the desert. Because the desert in the bible is a time of purification, its purpose is to help Israel know the Lord as he is. To understand they have everything they need in God, Israel needs to have anything redundant, wrong, or tainted in them and around them stripped away. All the misconceptions, lies, and corrupt ideas of how God is need to come to light and be rectified. So in the wilderness Israel experiences an intimate time with their Lord and every time he provides for them it's a tangible revelation of his goodness. Every time he drives this truth deeper into their hearts: He is the provider of all good things and being dependent on him is a blessing, not enslavement, and leads to perfect freedom, not to subjugation.

The desert is also a test to see where I am at in the process to freedom. A chance to reflect and consider God's many miracles and the relationship he is building between us. In close dependence on him, stripped from all misconceptions, lies, and corrupt ideas, I can begin to see who he truly is and through that who I am. Here in the wilderness, stripped of anything redundant, wrong, and tainted, it becomes apparent how deeply I know God, how much of me I already put in his hands, and which aspects of my life I still hold back. And while he is working on my heart and drawing me close to his, my needs are met with Manna, God's constant basic supply.

The desert is also a time of extremes. One day Israel is celebrating Pharaoh's defeat, the next day they are starving in the wilderness. One day they are living in an oasis, the next day they suffer thirst in barren lands. You need a constant, unchanging, unending basic supply to endure times like these. The desert is not a time to get rich, to store, or prepare. Manna is not supposed to be stored to get me through the winter, but rather it is supposed to free me from the daily worries so I can concentrate on the process of purification and growing closer to God. Even if the time in the desert becomes a difficult, draining struggle, I can be certain, my basic needs will be cared for, and I can focus on getting closer to God than ever before.

The desert is not the Promised Land. Manna is not the life in abundance God wants to give us. It is good to remember that, especially when the time in the desert gets long. God does not want us to adjust to the wilderness and settle for just the basic supply. He wants to prepare us for life in the Promised Land, life in his abundance. Manna in the desert is a miracle, but it only accompanies the purification process, it lets us last. It is God's constant, unchanging provision, built into the process of stripping away anything wrong and drawing us closer to him, so that we know himself and ourselves better than ever before. Until we reach the borders of the Promised Land, when the Manna will stop.

I grew up in a lively church, accustomed to having Sunday service and at least one other type of church meeting per week. Sunday school, children's choir, youth group, or bible school. My relationship with God was more or less a shared experience, something that mainly happened in groups and prepared events. So during my time in the desert, part of my purification process was to learn to walk with God without anyone to lead me into worship, without anyone preparing a sermon for me, without anyone creating an atmosphere for the Holy Spirit to move freely. It had started with a longing and the resolution to follow God more closely, which had led me to a new life in a new town, with a new career, and without a local church to attend. This new life had me serve somebody else's vision whilst preparing me for my own, and demanded everything from me. Actually, it seemed like it demanded far more than I had to give. And my two usual ways to recharge were now unattainable: My family was three hours away and I had no spiritual family either. The rare occasions I was able to attend a church service seemed like islands in uncharted waters. Until God put a stop to that, too.

I suddenly found I just couldn't share in the experience anymore, wasn't touched by the music anymore, couldn't feel the Holy Spirit moving anymore, and instead of speaking to me through the preacher, God started to talk to me about other things during the sermon. Only four years before that, I had found it so unbearable to endure just one evening without experiencing God's presence in a youth service, I had cried the whole night to get that feeling back. Now began ten years where my relationship with God was reduced to talking to him on my own and the occasional prayer with a friend. Before, I would have thought this would make me drift away from faith, would let my relationship with the Heavenly Father decrease without a platform to share and celebrate it. Instead God was stripping away anything non-essential and thus drew me into a much deeper relationship, into a much more trusting dependence, and into a much stronger faith. Because I had no one else, I learned to go to him first with anything I needed. Because the people I would usually talk to, reflect and share thoughts with were not reachable on a daily basis, I learned to talk to him about anything and stay in constant communication with him. Because I was overwhelmed by so many things in my life and by my job, I learned to ask him for daily strength, guidance, and help, and saw him answer every prayer.

Just like Israel in the desert I sometimes felt drained, exhausted, and even afraid whether I would last through this challenging time. Just like Israel I was forced to rely on God alone because everything else was stripped away. Just like Israel he drew me closer to himself. Just like Israel I got to know him as my provider. Just like Israel his constant, unchanging provision carried me through this time of purification and preparation. And just like Israel he led me through the desert and into my Promised Land, prepared and strengthened to now work towards and live in my vision.

That is the purpose of the desert and Manna: To draw us closer to God, see where we are at, have us grow in trust and faith, get purified and prepared for the Promised Land, all while we are carried through the challenges by his constant, unchanging provision. It might seem too much at times. It might feel like everything is stripped from you. It might seem like a long time of just basic provision. We might even lose sight of the coming Promised Land. But God is the same as he was and as he will be. Just like his people we cannot fall deeper than into his hands. And just like his people he wants to draw us close to him and reveal himself as the loving provider of all good things.

So, if you feel like your life is too much for you. If it seems like everything is being stripped away from you. If it feels like you are just barely getting by on only basic provision. If you fear you've lost sight of the Promised Land, don't despair. Look to God and open your heart to what he wants the time in the desert to be. He longs to draw you closer to himself. Longs to free you from all the misconceptions, lies, and corrupt ideas you might have about him. Longs to draw you into a closer dependence on him. Longs to show you, how deeply you know him, how much of yourself you already put into his hands, and which aspects of your life you still hold back. So that you, stripped from anything redundant, wrong, or tainted, can begin to see who God truly is and through that who you truly are. Dare to focus on him and know him closer. Don't fear you won't last, he will give you his constant, unchanging provision to endure the time in the wilderness. But also don't get too comfortable. The desert is not your Promised Land, not your vision, and Manna is not God's abundance. A time will come for you where you will see the fruits of the seeds you are sowing right now. And like I am every day, you will be grateful for everything you learned and saw God do in the desert.

If this speaks to you, look for him and his purpose behind your time in the desert. "Heavenly Father, I feel like I am in the desert right now. I am overwhelmed and fear I might not get through this. But I want to trust you. I want to know you like I have never known you before. Draw me closer, purify me, strip away all my misconceptions of you, and reveal yourself to me. I trust your provision and know, you are preparing me for the Promised Land. I put all of me into your hands once more."

In all of this you can rely on his provision. You won't fall deeper than into his hands and he will let bread rain from heaven to take care of you. His Manna will sustain you. It might come in the form of actual miracles of provision. It might come in the shape of a job you feel like you took just because you needed one, not because it was your true calling. It might come in the form of a friendship for the road that God put into your life just for a time. No matter what shape or form Manna will have for you, you can trust God will provide for you and carry you all the way through the desert. And he will draw you closer to himself than ever before.

God's perfect provision

The second five stanzas of the Dayenu, the "Five Stanzas of Miracles", perfectly exemplify God's goodness and love towards us. They show his caring heart, reveal him as our provider, as the source of all good things. They show us what we need to know about him. He is the way maker, splitting waters for us. He leads us through the sea on dry land. He drowns our oppressors behind us. He provides food, water, protection, and victory. He is carrying us through the desert, while he is drawing us close to himself and purifying us for the Promised Land. Where we will live in his abundance, in close dependence on him.

The Five Stanzas of Miracles also show me what my life with God can be like. With him there are no dead ends he cannot open up for me. He will always make a way I can walk on without stumbling, a road fitting my faith and trust in him. None of my old oppressors can touch me, for he will defeat them behind me. Wherever he leads me, he will provide for me, draw me into a closer dependence on him, and prepare me for the Promised Land. Where I will know him as the true source of all provision and the loving giver of all good things.

The five stanzas are also a guideline to see where I stand in the process of getting to know God as he really is. Whenever I get into a situation where there seems to be no way out, I can ask God: "Where am I right now? Do I need you to split the seas for me? Or do you want to invite me to put more of me into your hands? Do I need to remember how you will defeat my oppressors for me? Or do you want to teach me anew the freedom that lies in total dependence on you?"

No matter his answer, I will benefit from looking for God's purpose in any situation. Like Israel, I will experience an intimate time with my Lord and every time he provides for me it will be a tangible revelation of his goodness. And every time he will drive this truth deeper into my heart: He is the provider of all good things and being dependent on him is a blessing, not enslavement, and leads to perfect freedom, not to subjugation.

So, maybe you need God to make a way for you right now. Maybe you need reassurance that the road he made for you will be easy to walk without stumbling. Maybe you fear your past might soon catch up with you and you could really use a wave to drown your oppressors behind you. Maybe you never grasped before what it means to look to God for all your needs. Maybe you know you are in the desert right now and are worried whether or not you will be able to endure.

If any of this is true for you, I invite you to turn to God and ask him to reveal himself to you in a deeper way. Reach for that precious, important, life-altering revelation: God is the loving provider and true source of every good thing. Ask the Holy Spirit to teach you to understand God is good, wants to shower you with love, and answer any need you might have. Let this revelation change everything.

Grasping God as the only true source of all provision and every good thing will change where you will go for help. And understanding God as perfect goodness, who is all for you, will change how you approach him. Through Jesus, God's greatest gift of mercy and grace, we can

"approach God's throne of grace with confidence, so that we may receive mercy and find grace to help us in our time of need."
(Hebrews 4:16)

And there we will see all our needs met and our lives showered with goodness in abundance.

Fulfilment enough

The Five Stanzas of Closeness with God

After five steps out of slavery and five miracles of provision, here they are now. Shaken up, scared, mightily delivered, miraculously provided for, and victoriously protected. But still without much of a clue what all this is for. Israel has now seen God the mighty deliverer and God the loving provider. They slowly begin to grasp who this deity is that decided to be their God. But why? What purpose does he have for all of it? Where is he leading them? And what will a life in his hand be like? Up until now they have seen how he acts. They have yet to see his heart. That is what the last five stanzas of the Dayenu talk about. They show what it all comes down to in the end, show God's purpose for every step up until now, and show his motivation for the entire Exodus. Why he went to such lengths to provide us with a way into his perfect freedom, and why he revealed himself as the loving giver of all good things.

When God sent Moses to the Pharaoh for the first time, he told him to say:

"This is what the Lord, the God of Israel, says: 'Let my people go, so that they may hold a festival to me in the wilderness.'"
(Exodus 5:1)

It kind of seems like God told Moses to lie to Pharaoh. He always intended to free his people entirely. Why would he pretend he wants them to have a worship service in the desert instead? I don't think it was a lie. It was the absolute truth. God wanted to call them out of Egypt so they could worship him, encounter him, be with him, know him. For this is his motivation, his desire: communion, relationship, friendship. To restore his children to what Adam and Eve had been in Eden.

So after providing a way to step out of slavery and showing himself as the source of all security and provision, he teaches Israel how to build a relationship with him, how to establish a life in his hands. A life completely free because it is completely dependent on him. Again, it takes five steps, five things God institutes in his people to set them apart from all other civilizations in the world. Five distinct revelations of his goodness and love to grasp his purpose for us, and realize: he himself is the source of the fulfilment we long for.

Like Israel, we need God to not only break us free and take care of us, but also to fulfil us. We are made to be incomplete without him, we need him to fill this God-shaped, eternal hole in our souls. And just like before, we need God to provide this path to fulfilment himself, need him to, in his grace and goodness, offer us this relationship with him. Because we could never deserve it and never create it ourselves. In him alone we will find fulfilment, he alone makes a way for us to reach him, the source of all hope and happiness.

And again the example he gave us with his people shows us the five steps he will take to establish this deep relationship. Again, he extends this invitation to step into his dimension, into his kingdom, and accept his offer of grace. Again, he himself creates what we need, before we could ever deserve it. And, again, all we have to do is say yes.

If he had given us the Shabbat

The first thing God institutes among his people, to create a place of encounter and communion with him, actually happened long before the Exodus, in the second chapter of Genesis.

By the seventh day God had finished the work he had been doing; so on the seventh day he rested from all his work. Then God blessed the seventh day and made it holy, because on it he rested from all the work of creating that he had done. (Genesis 2: 2-3)

God blesses and sanctifies the seventh day and sets it apart as a day of rest, reflection, and relationship. It's the first day Man experiences in Eden. The first thing God wants Man to do is rest and enjoy creation with him. This shows his priorities. The relationship with him comes before work and ministry. God cements this institution of a rest-day with his newly freed people in Exodus 16:25-29, when he tells them, there won't be manna on the seventh day, but instead a double portion on the sixth day, providing for them all they need to rest on the seventh day. And further more in Exodus 20:8-11 when he commands them to keep the Shabbat holy. Before all the commandments of not killing, not stealing, and not lying, God makes a point of implementing a day of encounter and communion. Which, again, shows his priorities. In the Ten Commandments he first establishes himself as the God, who brought them out of Egypt, and forbids his people to worship other gods and take his name in vain. And then, before telling them how to behave, he first calls them unto himself by declaring his day of encounter and communion as holy. In Exodus 23:10-11 he decrees not only a rest-day per week for Man but also every seven years a year for the land to recover, for servants to be released, and for debts to be cancelled. And what will happen if Israel stops obeying these commandments?

> *I will scatter you among the nations and will draw out my sword and pursue you. Your land will be laid waste, and your cities will lie in ruins. Then the land will enjoy its Shabbat years all the time that it lies desolate and you are in the country of your enemies; then the land will rest and enjoy its Shabbats. (Leviticus 26: 33-34)*

The land gets to catch up on the Shabbats it missed because of the people's disobedience. That is the significance and value rest has in God's eyes: It's the first thing Man experiences in paradise, the first thing God commands us to keep and observe. He provides enough so we don't have to work to sustain us. Furthermore, we get to catch up on it if circumstances or even our own disobedience kept us from enjoying it.

Looking closely at how God's people still celebrate this special, God-given holy day, underlines what unique gift to us this day is. First of all, in the Jewish tradition the day starts in the evening with a dinner accompanied by prayers of thanksgiving and blessing. The whole family consciously turn their hearts and minds toward God by thanking him for his goodness and provision, past, present, and future. The father blesses his wife by reading Proverbs 31:10-31 (the praise of A Wife of Noble Character), his sons with the blessing of Ephraim and Manasseh, his daughters with the blessing of Sarah, Rebekah, Rachel, and Leah, and finally all of them together with the Priestly Blessing from Numbers 6:24-26. And then they enjoy rest and restoration during a good night's sleep, before spending the whole day together in God's presence.

What a precious institution this is! To be blessed every week! To have a well-established ritual to help putting the work-week with all its stress and demands behind you. To turn to God, rest, recharge, and enjoy relationships!

Gratitude, receiving and expecting good things, consciously focussing on times of rest and restoration, making time for reflection, family, and deep encounters: these are all techniques they teach in advanced work-life-balance classes to handle or avoid burn-out. This is God's gift to us. He simply presents us with it, it was the first thing he did, as soon as Man was created. Here you are, have a day of rest and keep it holy. You will be blessed if you do. Amazing, isn't he?

He still does this today. When I came to a point in my life and career when I decided I wanted to live entirely in God's hands, follow his plan for me, and do whatever he told me to do, the very first thing he did, was drawing me unto himself by giving me a trip to Israel. Which I didn't have to pay for and which changed my life. It was such a weird situation for me, because at the time I just had interviewed for a job, which I had to decline in order to go on the Israel trip. I remember my youth pastor trying to appeal to my conscience: "Well, it is entirely up to you and what you feel you should do. You have been unemployed for a while now. But you have to decide on your own whether you need a job or a vacation right now." Even though her thinly veiled opinion usually meant the world to me, I deeply felt drawn towards the Israel trip. So I followed my heart and took the trip, despite feeling the pressure to defend my illogical choice. As a result, I was changed. God revealed himself to me through the 'testimony of the stones'[4] and through the faith of his people. He showed me his love for Israel and by extension for me in a life-altering deep revelation, drew me closer to himself than ever before, and called me into ministry. So, as it turned out, I really did need that vacation more than a job, after all.

Working in hotels for the last 14 years I came to feel how much this rest day runs in our blood. In the service industry it is not uncommon to work stretches of up to nine days in a row, days off rarely coincide with the weekend, it is easy to lose count which weekday it actually is. It can get quite tiring. Again and again I experienced some days, where everything was somehow more exhausting and altogether harder than normal. And whenever I stopped to think why this day was so much less bearable, I would always find: it was the seventh workday in a row. Six days I would work as normal, the seventh day would be hardly tolerable, and the eighth day would be normal again. It was as if, on the seventh day, my whole body would try to tell me: "Wait a minute! This is wrong! Today should be different from the last six! Why are we still doing the same thing?" Every single time I worked a seventh day. Like clockwork. It is in our bones. God must have put it there.

I changed jobs and towns in October of 2018 and was still settling into my new life when, in early 2019, I got sick. Not terribly, just a little cold, followed by seven weeks of fatigue. As if someone had turned up the gravity to 400%.

---

[4] Following Jesus' statement in Luke 19:40 this phrase describes the feeling and event, when a person experiences God as intensely real in Israel. The stones of the land testify the truth of the Bible stories.

What had at first been diagnosed by the doctors as a little virus infection, turned out to be a little burn-out instead. To my doctor this was a good diagnosis, because he had pills for that, namely antidepressants. To me it was an appalling shock. I thought of myself as being self-aware and self-reflecting enough to know my own mind and soul. With burn-out being one of my foremost specialist subjects. But doctors make bad patients, as do counsellors, apparently. It took me 24 hours and quite a bit of talking and thinking things through to sort out my thoughts, mainly because I didn't understand what could have overwhelmed me so. My new life right now was a breeze compared to what I had had to carry, give, and serve at my previous job, both physically and spiritually. Now I was relaxed, never overstrained, never over-exhausted. So why did I burn out now, not the year before? Then, I had been struggling due to the depression phase of mourning my father's passing. Then, I had felt enormous pressure and guilt not only to perform during work hours but to minister and serve as an evangelist and then teacher to the new disciples in my time off. So why now and not then?

It was my mom who brought up the verse in Leviticus 26 to me: "Well, God says the land needs to catch up on the Shabbats it missed due to the people's disobedience, so why wouldn't you need that as well? For the last eleven years you couldn't enjoy a guilt-free Shabbat, its high time you catch up on some of them." She was right. I needed the catch-up. I needed to revisit these past eleven years. I needed to reflect on them and think them through. I needed to be thankful for some things and debunk other things. I needed to let them go, needed to recharge, and receive God's blessing and provision. That's what my bones tried to tell me by turning up the gravity to 400%: "We have had enough. Now it is time to do something different. Seek an encounter with God." Which was just what I needed. What a relief and restoration it was!

Of all the Jewish traditions I grew up with, the Shabbat was the first and the most conscientiously observed. Funnily enough, it had been my mother's idea, not my father's. In an attempt of having at least one evening of the week where Dad would come home from work early, she suggested celebrating Shabbat. Which was something after Dad's heart, of course, so it was easy for him to make it a priority. Thus, the tradition began, even though we five kids didn't like it, and showed that whenever we could. Unperturbed Dad suffered our disrespect, our jokes, and our sarcastic eye rolls, and soldiered on celebrating God's holy day with a family that looked down on his "weird little hobby". To this day I don't fully understand how he could endure all our fighting against what to us was merely a way to boringly prolong a dinner but to him was so precious. It is a true testament to Dad's devotedness and unrelenting faithfulness to his conviction that the precepts of the Lord are right and give joy to the heart. He just kept on living his faith and relationship with God before our eyes, unflinching and unyielding. And even though we didn't acknowledge it and without even realizing it, we learned that the Shabbat is the Holy Day, a day of thanksgiving, blessing, rest, restoration, reflection, and relationship.

The true value of being allowed to grow up with this wonderful God-given tradition I only started to realize after my father died. And it seems he had been expecting us to come around to it because when my mom got home from my father's memorial service in Berlin, she found a book while tidying containing the Shabbat liturgy and prayers in Hebrew and German. My father had had a similar book for decades, but this new one did not only contain the Hebrew version with a translation, but also a phonetic Hebrew version in Latin script. Dad had ordered this new book because he knew full well, none of us could read the Hebrew letters; he knew Mom would need the transliteration.

It was a very special, caring gift, showing Dad's astonishing foresight and love for us. And it fell into Mom's hands just in time. Only a few days before we had tried to stumble through the Shabbat ceremony by just piecing together what we could remember in a group effort. The result had been a sort of patchwork of prayers with bits of blessings, all clumsily stitched together with laughter, tears, and threads of memories. Growing up, we had often babbled along with Dad reading the verses, mostly while mockingly rolling our eyes. Now we really tried to get it right and everyone pitched in, trying to compile as much as we could of the liturgy. The outcome was far from perfect, but I am convinced it would have filled Dad's heart to the brim.

Here, in the community[5] I live and work in, we have a tradition. Every Wednesday evening we have dinner together, starting with the Holy Communion and ending with the minister praying the Priestly Blessing over the congregation. This is as close as I get to a Shabbat ceremony nowadays. So when I attended this celebration for the first time, it made me a little sad. It had me thinking about, and comparing it to, our family Shabbat. Happy memories of precious blessings, interspersed with the sadness of knowing, I will never hear my father pray for me again. And then the Holy Spirit made me an immeasurably dear present: While our pastor prayed the

---

[5] The Community for the Unity of Christians in Schloss Craheim near Schweinfurt, Germany

Priestly Blessing over us, I simultaneously heard my father's voice pray the same prayer in Hebrew in my spirit. I will treasure that memory forever. Just as I will treasure my father's blessing in my life forever.

But can I tell you about my absolute favourite Shabbat of all time? It's the one that began on the evening of Jesus' crucifixion. While Jesus stepped into the realm of the dead, defeated the death I deserved for my sin, and conquered Satan for all eternity, the world got a day of rest and restoration in the Father's arms. What an incredible mercy and grace! He truly did EVERYTHING for me, saved me entirely and completely, I didn't have to do anything. I couldn't have done anything. I can rest in him, while he protects me. I can rest in him, while he provides for me. I can rest in him, while he conquers death for me. I can rest in him, while he fulfils me. I can rest in him. Now and forever.

Maybe you never had a family ceremony of heralding in the Holy Day of Rest. Maybe you never heard your father blessing your mother, your siblings, and yourself. Maybe you have no cultivated tradition to observe a day off in God's presence. Maybe you don't even think much about God on your weekends. Maybe you never knew God's priorities regarding rest, restoration, reflection, and relationships. Maybe you never even gave them much thought. Maybe you know all this but have to admit to not keeping this Holy Day really holy lately. Or maybe you have difficulty trusting God to provide a double portion for you so you can enjoy a guilt-free Shabbat. Well, let me tell you, the need for rest runs in our blood to this day. And God's gift of this Holy Day is available to each and every one of us. He longs to bless us, longs to draw us toward himself, longs for us to spend the day in his presence, longs to give us fulfilling rest, reviving restoration, and meaningful relationships. He knows us, he knows we need all this to keep our lives in a good balance. That's why he wants to give it to us. All we need to do is to, once again, accept his wonderful gift. Set the seventh day apart as the Holy Day of rest, where we come to God with thanksgiving and receive his blessing, provision, and fulfilment in his presence. You don't need to strictly follow the whole Shabbat liturgy, but it helps to have your own little evening ritual to consciously turn your heart and mind toward God with thanksgiving. So you can start into the rest day with open hands to receive the blessing of the Heavenly Father and enjoy the place he established for you. A place to deeply encounter him and have fulfilling communion with him.

"Thank you, Heavenly Father, for creating a special place for you and me by setting apart the Shabbat as a day of rest, restoration, and relationship. Please forgive me my disobedience, my neglect, and contempt toward your Holy Day. Forgive me that I so often played fast and loose with my own strength and with my own need for rest and your fulfilment. From now on, I will not call ordinary anymore what you have called holy. From now on I will trust you to give me a double portion so I can enjoy a guilt-free Shabbat. I will set the seventh day apart as a day to encounter you, to rest in your presence, to receive your fatherly blessing, and to grow in the knowledge of your love for me. You are the source of my fulfilment. Please teach me to establish this precious day in my life and family."

The blessing God laid on his Holy Day and on those who observe it is written down in Leviticus 26:2-13.

"Observe my Shabbat and have reverence for my sanctuary. If you follow my decrees and are careful to obey my commands, I will send you rain in its season, and the ground will yield its crops and the trees their fruit. Your threshing will continue until grape harvest and the grape harvest will continue until planting, and you will eat all the food you want and live in safety in your land. I will grant peace in the land, and you will lie down and no one will make you afraid. I will remove wild beasts from the land, and the sword will not pass through your country. You will pursue your enemies, and they will fall by the sword before you. Five of you will chase a hundred, and a hundred of you will chase ten thousand, and your enemies will fall by the sword before you. I will look on you with favour and make you fruitful and increase your numbers, and I will keep my covenant with you. You will still be eating last year's harvest when you will have to move it out to make room for the new. I will put my dwelling place among you, and I will not abhor you. I will walk among you and be your God, and you will be my people. I am the Lord your God, who brought you out of Egypt so that you would no longer be slaves to the Egyptians; I broke the bars of your yoke and enabled you to walk with heads held high."

In other words: living in his freedom through perfect security, unfailing provision, and everlasting fulfilment. It all begins with treasuring his Holy Day of rest, restoration, and relationship as much as he does. If we start there, we will see his blessings follow. And they will be perfect, unfailing, and everlasting.

If he had brought us before Mount Sinai

The second thing God institutes among his people to create a place of encounter and communion with him is his eternal covenant with them. For weeks they have been travelling, wandering through desert and wilderness. For weeks they have seen miracle after miracle. This God of their forefathers, who is so much more mighty and awe-inspiring than everything they experienced so far, leads them on and on as a pillar of cloud and fire, farther and farther away from everything they knew. At last, the Israelites reach Mount Sinai, where they set up camp. As he did many times before, Moses talks to God and tells the people what the Almighty said. This God, who just rescued them with a mighty hand, who they fear and don't completely trust, reveals his heart to them and gives the first answer to the question of why he did what he did:

'You yourselves have seen what I did to Egypt, and how I carried you on eagles' wings and brought you to myself. Now if you obey me fully and keep my covenant, then out of all nations you will be my treasured possession. Although the whole earth is mine, you will be for me a kingdom of priests and a holy nation.' (Exodus 19: 4-6)

That is what God truly wants: a treasured possession, a kingdom of priests and a holy nation. Being his, ministering at a God-given altar, a place for God to reveal himself. Becoming the example for the entire world to see what it is like to live in the close, fulfilling relationship we were made for. He wants to create a place of encounter and communion with him, so we can be his friends again, just like Adam and Eve were in Eden. To establish a place where we can live in his perfect freedom and provision again, and experience his perfect fulfilment.

Here, at Mount Sinai, it all comes down to the root and core of God's character: relationship. To be his, or not to be his, that is the question. He lays before them his covenant, his commitment to them, all his promises, all his heart. He indisputably shows them where he stands and gives them the chance to take a stand themselves. To say yes to his covenant and become his people. God shows up in person to this encounter, draws as close to them as he possibly can get without them perishing in his holiness. And he asks them: "Will you be mine?" How could they refuse? Unanimously they answer: "Yes, we want to be yours."

But what is this covenant he offers them? What is the core of this promise? The answer to that is found by looking into the Ark of the Covenant, the gold-covered wooden chest containing everything this alliance with God signifies. First, God places the stone tablets with the commandments in there, the law of the covenant, the guidelines to follow if they want to be God's people. Then, he places a vessel filled with Manna in the Ark, God's heavenly provision. And lastly, he places Aaron's rod in it, the very rod that had started to blossom as a confirmation of God's calling Aaron and his offspring into priesthood. So God's covenant with his people promises his guidance, his provision, and his calling and authority. With the content of the Ark of the Covenant God basically says: I will guide you through life, I will provide for you, I will have you as mine. He wants to commit himself to his people as their source of protection, provision, and fulfilment.

What fascinates me most about this part of the story, though, is that God offers them the covenant. He does not say: "Well, you saw what happened to Egypt because they were against me. You've got the same thing coming if you don't do as I say." No, he introduces himself to his people, shows them, what he is willing to do to save, protect, and sustain them, and only after that, he asks them whether they would like to keep his covenant. He lovingly asks: "I long to be your God, do you want to be my people?"

Again we see this longing for relationship, for encounter. At Mount Sinai it is important to God that all the people should hear his voice, not just Moses. He wants to be known, wants every last one of them to encounter him. After all he did for them, it is still entirely their choice to keep the covenant or not. This love leaves me speechless. It is utterly mind-blowing.

And it is also exactly what is needed for a deep, fulfilling relationship. Just like in the very beginning while planting the Tree of Knowledge, God puts our will above his own again, so we can be his equal. So we can be free to love him back. God's restraint and commitment build the perfect foundation to establish the fulfilling relationship we were made for and need so very much. And it takes our commitment, our yes to his covenant, to enter into this relationship.

I remember once, when I was about 17 or 18, Dad and I had been horseback riding and were driving back home. I was in charge of music and had picked a contemporary R&B album I liked. Interspersed with the songs it featured little clips, recorded in a high school classroom, of teenagers talking about love. At some point one of them said, in a laid-back all-knowing sort of way: "Love is just a feelin'…", which my father then copied when he said: "No, love is a decision…". This has stuck with me ever since. And I see the truth in that statement, whenever I see God's love for me. He doesn't love me because I am lovable, he loves me because he decided to do so. Because he is love. He can't not love me.

Whenever I find myself somewhere I never wanted to be, stuck in some horrible sin, disgraced and bound, doubting whether God still loves me, I hear my father's voice: "Love is a decision…" A decision God made before even creating the world. A decision he will never regret. A decision born out of his very being and completely unswayed by my actions. Again and again, all through the Bible, God stands by his covenant with his people, underlines it, repeatedly offers it to them, reinforces it, and even expands it, calling it the new covenant to include us, the gentiles.

When God took me on the life-changing trip to Israel, the greatest revelation he gave me was his unchanged, undiminished love for his people. It was like he opened a door to his heart and, for a moment, all I could see was how he will eternally honour his covenant with Israel, unflinching and unyielding. The sheer fact that the state of Israel even exists, shows how little God has given up on his promise to his people. The fact that the Israeli army is by far the most successful army in the world, shows how much God still fights for them. The fact that over 20% of Nobel Prize recipients are of Jewish heritage, while they should only make up 0,2% if the recipients were a representative cross section of the world, shows how undiminished God's blessing lies on the Israelites to this day. He never backed out of his covenant with them. He never will. He never stopped being their God and having them as his people. He never will.

In the New Testament, the only new thing about his covenant that could justify calling it thus is that now, through Jesus, we gentiles are invited in as well. By Jesus becoming the eternal Passover lamb, our eternal priest, and the eternal temple to encounter the Heavenly Father, he did not replace the covenant, he fulfilled it. Before, Jesus' position in God's covenant with us was held by three placeholders. The Passover lamb was established to atone for sin and free from death, reminding God of the Lamb to come. The anointed priest was appointed as an intermediary between the people and God, reminding him of the Priest to come. The temple was built as a place of deep encounter with God, reminding him of the Temple to come. Jesus fulfilled the covenant by replacing the placeholders, and opened it up for all mankind. But the core remains unchanged. God is still saying, to Israel and anyone who is willing to hear: "I will guide you through life, I will provide for you, I will have you as mine. I long to be your God, do you want to be my people?" And all we have to do to enter into this holy, unchanging, undiminished covenant with him, is to say yes.

This yes can be repeated as often as God repeats his offer to us. In fact, it has to. Every single day I am challenged by my fallen nature to stumble once again, and drawn by my spirit to hang on to God once again. His covenant with me stands, unfailing. It is I who has to say yes to it, sometimes minute by minute. But every time I do, God draws me deeper into his presence, his dimension, his kingdom. And deeper into his perfect freedom.

No wonder it is an intense encounter Israel experiences at Mount Sinai. After Moses brought their yes to him, God descends upon the mountain to encounter the entire people. They prepared for it, consecrated themselves, so they might not die in his holiness. Like a fiery thundercloud he dwells on the mountaintop, inspiring awe in the people below. They all experience about as much closeness with God as they can survive. The new alliance with the Lord is celebrated with a sacrifice and Moses sprinkles the people with the offering's blood, sealing the covenant. Then Moses alone is called up into the cloud to receive God's ordinances.

He stays up there for forty days and forty nights. Meanwhile Israel is getting restless. Moses is gone for so long, they assume he must have died in God's holiness. They don't want to wait any longer, so the people go to Aaron and demand he make them a god they can worship and follow. Aaron, in turn, doesn't wait either. He collects golden jewellery from everyone, melts the gold down, and makes it into an idol shaped like a calf. He builds an altar to sacrifice to this god and the people hold a large festival of idolatry with food, drink, and general revelry.

Of all the missteps Israel takes on their journey with God, this one is significant to me for two reasons: first of all because Aaron, despite being front and centre in all this, doesn't get struck down for it afterwards. That, to me, makes it feel like God was expecting it to happen or as if Aaron did what he was supposed to do. And I think, if he did what he was supposed to do, then it was for the benefit of the example God makes of Israel with the whole story of the Exodus. Secondly, because of the material this golden calf was fashioned out of. This jewellery was very probably a huge part of the treasures the Israelites were given by the Egyptians before they left slavery. In their eagerness to have a god to worship and follow, they turn the treasures from the land of their oppression into an idol.

Similarly, I have seen a lot of people in God's family whose ministry, originating from the victory over their oppression, turned into a false god itself. They accepted God's grace in form of the treasures of the land of their oppression, and mistook it as the reason why he had saved them in the first place. So their value, righteousness, and salvation were now tied to their ministry and success. Thus, they started worshipping their own calling instead of the one who was calling their hearts to him.

When I was in my teens, I went through such a process for the first time. I was just starting to see how God used me as a true friend for many of my peers. They came to me to talk things through, to hear some wise thoughts, or get insight by getting my outside perspective. But because I, too, mistook this as the reason God had saved me, and therefore as my solemn duty, I felt responsible and like a huge failure, every time someone didn't listen to or confide in me. If only I were a better friend, they would trust me more and live better lives. My calling defined my value and salvation, so I started to serve it rather than God. For I was convinced, God had called me for himself and into service, rather than calling me for me and unto himself. It's a toxic pit to fall into, but it is also something God wants and loves to free me from. His perfect freedom incorporates every shackle I put on myself, even if we had already been through the chapter of breaking me free from my false idols. He doesn't mind taking an extra turn, if that will take me closer to him in the end.

Just like the need for rest and restoration, I believe the need for the covenant with God runs in our blood. A need to know why he made us, saved us, and loved us. I believe Israel's restlessness at the foot of Mount Sinai came from the deep desire to finally answer to the awe and longing

God's mighty deeds inspired in them. They wanted a god to worship. Similarly, in view of Jesus' sacrifice and the Father's mercy, something in us wants to answer, wants to bow, wants to commit to him, wants to find ways to repay this indescribable grace. It is hard to understand and to bear that his decision to love us is irrevocable, unchanging, unrepayable, and shockingly one-sided. For us to just say yes to him and nothing more seems so small a reaction, seems like it cannot possibly be enough.

After God had freed me from idolizing my calling, I found myself longing to truly understand why God had made me, saved me, and loved me. And I found God peeling away one possible answer after the other. It was obvious to me that I wasn't worth the price he paid for me, especially in the state he found me in. I couldn't see anything in me that justified dying on the cross for. So I thought it must have been for the potential in me and tried to make his mercy for me worth his while. That led me straight into condemnation and depression, because I soon realized my inability to do or be anything worthy of the price he paid. Not only were my little acts of service nothing much to speak of, but I also found that even the things I tried to do for him were desperately dependant on him working in and through me. So what I thought I did was actually his work instead. Whenever the Spirit whispered to me about God's love he told me he had saved me, because he couldn't be without me. But what on earth could be so irreplaceable? And whatever it was would be something he put in me, so I, again, had nothing to bring to the table. So what did he see in me? In the end, God answered my question like this: "A piece of my heart is in you. I put it there, made you from it. I am not complete without you. I am missing a piece. The piece I took from myself to create an equal counterpart, who would love the same things I love, enjoy the same things I enjoy, and delight in the same things I delight in. That is why I made you out of my heart and bore you from my love. Because I wanted you to love creation with me. That makes you worth the price I paid for you. No, you cannot repay me, no, you cannot deserve my yes to you. All I long for is for you to say yes to me."

That's it. Nothing more, nothing less. I was made out of his love because he loves me, I am loved because he made me out of his love. It might seem hard to bear sometimes. It might get frustrating to fight the urge to repay the unrepayable. Our longing to become worthy of the price he paid might have led us to worship our calling rather than the one who is calling us to himself. Maybe his love for us is just too hard to grasp, his unchanging yes to us may be too hard to bear. But this covenant he offers us, that we can never repay and that we can add nothing to, is the very core of the Father's heart and love. To be his, or not to be his, is the only question we have to find an answer to.

Maybe you, too, struggle with accepting God's unrepayable love for you. Maybe you are still trying to find ways to prove worthy of his mercy. Maybe you are only now realizing how God is calling you for you and unto himself, rather than for himself and into service. Maybe the thought of simply being God's treasured possession is still too hard to wrap your head around. Maybe you never looked too closely at God's covenant before and, now that you have, feel, for the first time, the longing to do something in return. Then listen to this longing and dare to say yes to God's covenant with you. It will be the greatest step into perfect freedom you have ever taken.

"Heavenly Father, my mind is blown, my soul shaken to the core, my heart broken in the sight of your love for me!

I tried to deserve your sacrifice, tried to repay the price you paid for me. I worshipped my calling rather than answer you calling me to yourself. I mistrusted you, secretly accused you of having ulterior motives. But I want to know you as you are, to grasp your character, to receive your love, and to say yes to your covenant. Here I am, for the first time or once again. I want to be yours. Want to be your treasured possession forever. Holy Spirit, please teach me to follow God's guidance, to seek his provision, and to be his. Please draw me deeper into your presence, your dimension, your kingdom, and deeper into your perfect freedom."

Finally grasping that the price Jesus paid for me was unrepayable, freed me from the need to achieve my salvation through my works. It unmasked the lie that I might have to somehow earn God's love retroactively. It freed me from legalism, freed me from serving God with a false motivation. But it did not stop me from living for him. Rather it showed me the right motivation to follow him. Encountering his deep, unchanging, unending love for me made me want to love God the way he deserved it. So I looked at Jesus as a role model how to love the Father. And I realized, Jesus bore the humiliation, the whippings, and the cross, because he loved the Father so much, he couldn't bear God's heart to remain broken. He wanted to make a way for us to come back to God, for the pieces of God's heart to be restored to him. This is my motivation to serve in the kingdom of God: To love the Father like Jesus loved him, and therefore to help restore the pieces of God's heart to him. I want to see anyone I meet as a piece of God's heart, a piece he misses dearly. And I want to love God so much, I cannot bear his beautiful heart to be broken into pieces. At least, I wish I could be that person. I strive to be that person. But in this as in everything else, I have to accept: I can't do anything on my own and have to let the Holy Spirit do it instead. All I can do is say yes to his covenant, yes to his guidance, yes to his provision, yes to being his, and let him do the rest.

That is the relationship God's covenant invites us into. That is what we say yes to when we finally commit to be his. And our yes will draw us inevitably deeper into his presence, his dimension, his kingdom, and his perfect freedom.

If he had given us the Torah

The third thing God institutes among his people to create a place of encounter and communion with him, is part of his covenant. At Mount Sinai, after offering it to them, he gives them guidelines for this new alliance. Up until now Israel knew no other civilisation, no other legal system, no other philosophy, no other way of life than Egypt's. But God debunked and destroyed all of it before their eyes. So they really don't know how to be a people, nor how to build a civilisation, nor how to live healthily, nor how to cure diseases. They have no culture, no customs, no rituals, no traditions of their own, no guidelines to live a good life by. They need not worry, though, because this is all part of God's covenant with them. After encountering all the people at the foot of Mount Sinai and sealing his commitment to them and their yes to him, God calls Moses up to the mountaintop to give his ordinances. We are not just talking about the Ten Commandments here, not by a long shot. The laws Moses brings back to the people, handwritten by God on tablets of stone, contain everything a nation would need to know to live in peace, justice, health, and prosperity. They are far more than just rules how to sacrifice, repent, and receive mercy. They establish a whole legal system, containing marriage and divorce laws, inheritance laws, restitution laws, personal injury laws, livestock injury laws, property laws, and social securities and responsibilities. They offer instructions for healthy living, hygiene, nutrition, and housekeeping, covering everything from washing hands and treating rashes to getting rid of mould in your walls. Everything other civilisations had to work out through trial and error, through decades of philosophy and scientific research, God just gives to his people on a stone platter.

What an immeasurable mercy and grace is it to get taught how to live a good life! Millenia before Louis Pasteur Israel knows to wash their hands, centuries before all dieticians Israel knows to best just eat the muscle flesh of an animal. These are not laws to make you righteous by living an immaculate life. These are God's guidelines to his blessing. The commandments are an enormous gift, once more showing God's love for his people. Like the Shabbat and his covenant, he gives this gift before the Israelites even know they need it. And like the Shabbat and his covenant, this gift sets Israel apart from all other nations in the world. These laws still build the foundation for many of the legislations in the world today, proving the wisdom behind them and showing the eternal consistency of the word of God.

No wonder that practicing Jews celebrate receiving the Torah every year by joyfully dancing through the streets with the scrolls, singing songs of thanksgiving and praise for God's amazing love and grace. So much do they rejoice in God's mercy of giving them rules to live a blessed life. How it must have torn Jesus' heart to pieces whenever he met someone shackled by the merciless interpretation of his Father's love-filled guide through life by people like the Pharisees. How it must sadden him to this day to see Christians calling the old law the opposite of grace and love, instead of an expression of them. Because that is what they truly are. They are God saying: "I love you, so I don't want you to seek false hope, false security, and false fulfilment with idols. I love you, so I don't want you to hate each other, be jealous of each other, or destroy each other. I love you, so I don't want you to do anything that would be bad for you. I love you, so I want you to be good. I love you, so whenever you cannot be good, I'll provide a way for you to repent and receive my mercy. I love you, so every sacrifice you bring for your atonement will remind me of the sacrifice I will bring to forever wash you clean and pay the price for your sin."

The laws are actually not entirely new at this point. The fact that Adam and Eve hid from God after eating the fruit, shows their guilty conscience. We see the same thing when we read about Cain murdering Abel and becoming defensive towards God. That can only mean one thing, at least to me: God already instilled his laws in Man at the moment of creation. Our conscience tells us wrong from right. It's there to steer us towards his blessing. God's laws are written on our hearts.

We need these guidelines to his blessing. They teach us about God's character and goodness. We can learn so much about his unending faithfulness, when we look at how much he doesn't want us to be unfaithful to one another. We can learn so much about his steadfast justness, when we look at how much he doesn't want us to be unjust to one another. We can learn so much about his immeasurable generosity, when we look at how much he doesn't want us to be ungenerous to one another.

When I was growing up our refrigerator in the kitchen was home to a large planner, consisting of six sheets of paper, one for every day of the week, excluding Sundays. Each sheet showed the class schedules for me and my siblings and underneath the chores we had to do that day. We all had to take out trash once a week, do the dishes once a week, buy groceries once a week, and clean one of the common rooms, like the living room, the kitchen, or the bathrooms once a week. With five children in the family, that totted up to quite a bit of help around the house, or so I thought back then. Of course, with five children in the family, that was far from being enough help. When friends from school saw this planner and how many chores I had to do, they would oftentimes pity me, saying they never had to help. This usually made me pity myself in return, resenting my Mom for making us work so much. It seemed so unfair that my friends could enjoy their childhoods, while I had to be so grownup and do housework. Until I went on a school trip in third grade and was the only one who knew how to make a bed. Then I realised, my mother didn't treat us as servants but taught us to be competent human beings, capable to deal with life. I love her for that.

Just like Adam and Eve in Eden, we sometimes think of God's laws as restrictions, harsh limitations to our self-determination, and overlook the glorious truth: these laws are for us, for our very best! They are the boundaries he gave us to live a life in his perfect freedom, given to us on a stone platter, so we don't hurt ourselves or one another. They are teaching us to be competent human beings, capable of loving one another and God.

In eighth grade I had my first chemistry class. Our teacher was our deputy headmaster, quite a scary looking, authoritative man. The first lesson we had with him he spent by telling us his rules. In a calm but daunting manner he simply listed his punishment for each and any transgression a group of teenagers might commit. It was intimidating to say the least. But it laid the foundation for the best class in my entire life at school. No other teacher before and since managed to teach me as much. Because we knew what would be coming for us, nobody dared to do anything. And because misbehaving was so absolutely out of the question, we followed the lessons far more attentively then in all the other classes combined. Only once in our two years with this teacher did one of my classmates break a minor rule by chewing gum. He was immediately found out and quickly removed the gum, fearing the worst. But the only thing he had to endure was a long, intimidating stare of judgement from our teacher. No punishment. It was not necessary, because we knew it should have happened, and for some reason that was enough. It didn't undermine our teacher's authority in the slightest. We were on our best behaviour to the very last lesson. Our teacher's demeanour wouldn't allow anything else.

By instituting his laws beforehand, God sets the tone for the relationship with his people and lays the foundation for the nation he is building. They establish his standard for holiness, setting the bar high, in some cases even unreachable. But he knows his standard is unattainable. He knows, we will fail him and will need his intervention to save us from sin. That's why he put the laws of the Sin Offering in. Not because the blood of animals can change much regarding our sinful nature, but because every lamb sacrificed would remind him of the lamb to come. This is God's love and grace expressed in his laws. He gives us guidelines to his blessing and with them a way to get saved from our cursed nature: through the Blood of the Lamb.

His commandments are still as much part of his covenant with us as they were the day Israel received them. But by Jesus becoming the eternal Passover lamb, our eternal priest, and the eternal temple to encounter the Heavenly Father, he invites us to let him write them on our hearts anew. To restore our conscience to what it was in Eden. So we know in our hearts to follow his example, long for his holiness, and strive for purification. We need this restoration. Living in a fallen world muddles our perception of right and wrong, paints life grey with no way to measure black and white anymore.

In my early twenties I went on three summer outreach trips to the Ukraine with my youth group. The warm continental climate gives the country hot summers, even the nights don't get much cooler than the days. So native Ukrainians are usually very scantily clad. At the beach, all one piece bathing suits were worn by members of our group, the natives only wore bikinis, no matter what body type. And even in the air-conditioned shopping malls you saw women wearing less material than I would need to cover my face. What was shockingly revealing the first day, became commonplace after a week. So when we returned to Germany after two weeks, it was almost weird and then somehow relaxing to the eyes to see people without showing their midriff and upper thighs. Because we had adjusted our conscience to the Ukrainian norm, we had to readjust, when we returned home.

We all need God to readjust our conscience. Sometimes on a daily basis. Because we live in a fallen world and are very capable of rearranging our own worldview if need be. A pastor friend of mine has seen this human trait in action again and again, when doing outreach in red light districts. Most prostitutes stated they don't mind selling their bodies. Many even claimed they like it. But if asked whether it had always felt this way to them, they oftentimes broke down, saying how much they had despised the first jobs, how nauseating it had been, and how ashamed and debased they had felt afterwards. They had to harden their hearts and adjust their conscience to survive.

It can be a harrowing experience to find just how much my conscience already diverges from God's laws. To see what he initially wanted me to be and what I have become instead. When Israel returned from the Babylonian exile, the consequence of breaking God's covenant, and for the first time in generations heard the laws God had given them, they were shattered. Devastated by the realisation of their disobedience and unfaithfulness, they cried and grieved in sackcloth and ashes. The laws, differing so much from the state of affairs, must have put a crushing weight on their hearts. Ezra, the priest who read out the laws to the people, and Nehemiah, the governor, held on to the Godly perspective, though. They told them to rejoice and have a feast instead.

Nehemiah said, "Go and enjoy choice food and sweet drinks, and send some to those who have nothing prepared. This day is holy to our Lord. Do not grieve, for the joy of the Lord is your strength." (Nehemiah 8: 10)

The joy of the Lord is our strength in all this. To rejoice in the fact that God loves us so much, he gave us wonderful guidelines to his blessing. To be amazed by God's grace, instead of broken down by shame and condemnation. To hold on to the truth that God is the loving giver of all good things, daily offering us his covenant and his salvation. To marvel at his goodness and mercy, rather than focussing on our failures and shortcomings.

Sometimes when we find ourselves devastated by the realisation of our sin, shame and condemnation keep us from turning to God. They seem appropriate, because they usually come disguised as a broken heart and humility. We should be broken-hearted by our sin, we should feel humble, anything else would be presumptuous and prideful. So we beat ourselves up instead of seeking God's mercy. And we feel right to do so. We should have known better by now, we say. We need to grovel to prove we are sorry, we think. Maybe we even doubt God will forgive us this time. Let me tell you, this shame is a very toxic form of pride and arrogance. While pride says I don't need God, his forgiveness, and Jesus' sacrifice to save me, shame says God, his forgiveness, and Jesus' sacrifice are not enough to save me. Believing the lie of condemnation is like spitting in the face of the Crucified, saying he is not needed or not enough. Shame is calling him a liar.

We need Jesus' sacrifice. We are made to need him. There is no other way to the Father. Also, his sacrifice is enough, even for that one horrible, disgusting sin you struggle with. And thinking we should have known better, is the same as priding ourselves to be capable of following God's law without the help of the Holy Spirit. We are not. We need the Holy Spirit to convict us and to lead us into the truth. We cannot possibly grasp God's infinite mercy and grace with our finite mind. 'But if God knew, what I did this time, he would turn away from me for sure!' Do you think that sometimes? Then I've got news for you. Our sin does not shock God. Our failures do not surprise him. Our confession is not news to him. He knows. And he knows all the other horrible things you haven't even realised about yourself, too. So like Nehemiah did with Israel, the Holy Spirit longs to invite us to stop grieving and rejoice in God's goodness instead. To look up to him, instead of down on ourselves. His salvation is far more about him, than it could ever be about me. The prodigal son did not stay with pigs, shattered by the realisation of his sin. He ran to the Father, because he knew about his goodness and longed for his salvation. While he was merely hoping to be forgiven but couldn't be exactly sure, we have the great privilege of having seen God's mercy and grace in action and having heard of his faithfulness and unwavering commitment to his covenant with us. We have his promise of salvation in Jesus. There is no room for shame and condemnation left.

Maybe you are shattered by the realisation of your own sin. Maybe you see how much you adjusted your conscience to survive. Maybe you have never seen God's love and grace in his laws. Maybe you still see them as harsh limitations to your self-determination. Whatever it is you struggle with now, let me tell you this: God loves you immeasurably. He wants to give you the very best. He instituted his laws as guidelines to his blessing. He knows they are unattainable. He knows you need his salvation. He knows you need Jesus' sacrifice. He knows your conscience needs restoration. He knows you need the Holy Spirit to convict you and lead you into the truth. He is neither appalled nor repulsed by you. Before creation he decided to love you, he won't stop now. He is standing with open arms. Look up to him, not down on yourself. He is standing with open arms.

I tell you, there is rejoicing in the presence of the angels of God over one sinner who repents. (Luke 15: 10)

If your heart draws you to turn to him again, just tell him. "Father, I have never seen your love in your laws. I believed them to be merciless restrictions for too long. I long to be guided towards your blessing. Renew my heart and mind, restore my conscience. I confess, I doubted the necessity and power of Jesus' sacrifice. I have looked down on myself rather than up to you. Please reveal to me the love in your laws and the power in your sacrifice. Please lead me into the truth. I receive the gift of your covenant and your guidelines to your blessing. I long to know you as you are. Reveal yourself to me once more."

It is immeasurably precious to learn to look up at the Father instead of down on yourself. To seek his love and grace in his ordinances, and letting him establish his love-filled laws at the foundation of our relationship with him. It will lead us into a life in his presence, his dimension, his kingdom, and his perfect freedom. And will bring us his perfect fulfilment.

If he had brought us into the land of Israel

The fourth thing God institutes for his people to establish a place of encounter is to give them a land, a country of their own to live in peace and prosperity. A land God promised Abraham at their very first encounter and several times after that. On numerous occasions God describes the life Israel will have in the Promised Land, a land flowing with milk and honey, a land of endless provision. A land they did not cultivate, with cities they did not build. Where they will eat from vineyards and olive groves they did not plant. (Joshua 24:13)

He promises rain in its season, more harvest than they can eat, and peace in the land. He promises, he will remove any danger, give them success in warfare, let them be fruitful and grow into a striving nation. (Exodus 26:3-11)

And best of all: he will dwell among them. He will be their God, who delivered them from their oppressors and enabled them to walk with their heads held high. (Exodus 26:12-13)

It's a good and very necessary thing that God revealed himself to Israel as their provider during their time in the desert, because this Promised Land has an interesting little quirk. It needs God's intervention for all that milk and honey to flow:

The land you are crossing the Jordan to take possession of is a land of mountains and valleys that drinks rain from heaven. It is a land the Lord your God cares for; the eyes of the Lord your God are continually on it from the beginning of the year to its end. So if you faithfully obey the commands I am giving you today—to love the Lord your God and to serve him with all your heart and with all your soul— then I will send rain on your land in its season, both autumn and spring rains, so that you may gather in your grain, new wine and olive oil. I will provide grass in the fields for your cattle, and you will eat and be satisfied. (Deuteronomy 11:11-15)

Again, this longing for relationship. This desire to be closely involved with his people. Far more than just a place he describes a life with them, a life completely dependent on him. A life where things will come easy to them, where they will see success without exhaustion, fruit without struggle, and peace without force. Where they will be like fish in water, exactly as they are made to be. Living approximately like Adam and Eve in Eden. All made possible by living in complete dependence on God, and therefore in his perfect security, unfailing provision, and everlasting fulfilment.

Living in the Promised Land in his hand, God sets Israel as an example for a life in his presence and grace. So all the world will see what a relationship with the Almighty should be. All the 40 years in the desert they walked with God's promise to their forefathers in their hearts. With his promise to bring them into the land of his rest. This is Israel's calling. This is why God made the childless Abraham into a great people as numerous as the stars in the sky and as the sand on the seashore. This is how his descendants become a blessing to all nations on earth. As an example for the world, as the place where God chose to dwell and reveal himself.

That is what God still has for me as well: a calling, a life in his hand, like a fish in water, as much like living in Eden as possible. That is what Jesus was talking about in his parables: his Kingdom come. Dwelling right at the source of every good thing and all life. In the hands of a God who is neither bound by location nor the laws of nature to answer my need. And who loves me and longs to shower me with abundant blessings. So that I, too, may become an example of the relationship we are made for and a blessing to the world, and my heart a place for God to reveal himself. Just like Israel before me, God leads me into my Promised Land through desert and wilderness. So that I, too, may know him as the only source of security, provision, and fulfilment beforehand. And won't see my Promised Land as the place to serve and finally work off the debt God's grace has put me in. We need to grasp beforehand that our Promised Land is not a sacrifice to offer, a heavy burden to carry, a duty or responsibility. It is a place to live in the rhythm of God's heartbeat and let his light shine through us into the world.

To live a life in his presence and in dependence on him, he first draws us to himself. He takes his time to eradicate our slave's mindset and plant the knowledge of our true value in him into our hearts. He doesn't mind taking an extra turn to make sure we truly know him before leading us into our Promised Land. That is the blessing of Moses' intercession for Israel:

"If your Presence does not go with us, do not send us up from here. How will anyone know that you are pleased with me and with your people unless you go with us? What else will distinguish me and your people from all the other people on the face of the earth?" And the Lord said to Moses, "I will do the very thing you have asked, because I am pleased with you and I know you by name."
(Exodus 33:15-17)

To reveal himself to us, that we may truly know him, is and always will be God's first priority. By drawing us to himself he prepares us for our life in our Promised Land. He teaches us to look to him alone for all security, provision, and fulfilment, and establishes the close, meaningful relationship we were made for. Then, and only then, will he lead us into our calling, our Promised Land.

After 40 years in the desert, after seeing God save them, protect them, provide for them, and bless them, Israel is finally ready to follow him into Canaan. By now, the old generation has died out, the people's faith and trust in God is founded on all the miracles they have seen him do in the desert. They know: if he is determined to give them the Promised Land, there will be no one who could keep him from it. Neither city walls nor giant soldiers can stand up to the Lord of Hosts when he fights for his people. Step by step, he guides them, bit by bit they take over the lands. God drives their enemies out of the country before them, just as he promised.

"I will send my terror ahead of you and throw into confusion every nation you encounter. I will make all your enemies turn their backs and run. I will send the hornet ahead of you to drive the Hivites, Canaanites and Hittites out of your way. But I will not drive them out in a single year, because the land would become desolate and the wild animals too numerous for you. Little by little I will drive them out before you, until you have increased enough to take possession of the land." (Exodus 23:27-30)

He tears down strongholds like Jericho, has Israel destroy the altars of the local idols and declare him the sovereign God. Wherever they go to take possession of the land, Israel finds: God hands the Promised Land over to them easily. Only once Israel sees defeat in the process of conquering Canaan: because one soldier steals from the plunder God had devoted for total destruction. Israel deals with this sin ruthlessly and find themselves back in God's grace. Because they know him as the giver of all good things, they naturally turn to him for instructions and fighting strategies. Because they know he fights for them, they confidently take possession of lands, cities, vineyards, and olive groves. Because they know he is the only true God, they fearlessly tear down the altars of the local idols and declare the God of Abraham, Isaac, and Israel as the sovereign Lord. Because they know him, they believe his promise to give them this country as the land of his rest, as a life in his hands.

God still works just like this today. He doesn't save us just to lead us around in the desert. He wants to bring us into our own Promised Land, where we live in the rhythm of his heartbeat, like a fish in water. After drawing us to himself he wants to set us as an example of a life in his hands. That we become a blessing to the world by letting his light shine through us. He still leads us there step by step, tearing down strongholds in us and before us, driving our enemy out, and giving the lands into our hands.

Catherine received God's calling for her life within the first six months after giving her heart to Jesus. The vision he gave her would involve the treasures of the oppression she was still struggling with, her family, her business, and her whole trade. While she fixed her eyes on that calling and followed the Holy Spirit little by little to work towards it, she found the first several steps to take where to receive God's restoration and affirmation. He started to heal her old wounds, liberating her from old shackles, and replaced the lies she had believed about herself with his truth. After letting the Holy Spirit clean up her life she naturally looked for his guidance towards her calling.

At around that time I started working for her. God had prompted me to take that job after I had decided I wanted to live entirely in God's hands, follow his plan for me, do whatever he told me to do, and live wherever he would send me. I had not the slightest idea what God wanted me in Catherine's business for. And, looking back, I can see that was a good thing, because I would not have been able to do any of it. I only knew I would just be there for a certain time, and that it was not my vision but Catherine's I was serving. She and I became close praying partners, seeking the Holy Spirit to guide us step by step, to take possession of Catherine's Promised Land. It took longer than both of us had thought it would. But looking back it is so obvious why God worked as he did.

Just like he healed and purified Catherine, he started cleaning up her business next. We witnessed him taking down strongholds, both in us and around us. He had us destroy false idols, again both in us and around us. Certain employees quit their jobs after we started praying for God to put people after his heart in key positions. Department after department we put into God's hands in prayer and could see how easily he liberated them, changed the atmosphere, and with it the productivity. These prayer sessions, though always uniquely guided by the Holy Spirit, showed certain similarities. We usually went praying after the whole department had finished working for the day, which could mean 11pm in some cases. The Holy Spirit would tell us about the local spiritual authorities and the roots of their claims to the house. We would ask God to forgive the sins that had opened the doors for impure spirits. He would give us authority to cast them out and we would seal the area with anointing oil. And then God would turn the whole department on its head and the whole business into his house.

Meanwhile God gave Catherine a new product to develop that would use the treasures of her past oppression to help other people break free from similar struggles. During the different stages of development God kept working in both of us. Both Catherine and I got to know God on a deeper level, saw and grasped him as our provider and the source of our fulfilment, and experienced his comfort, healing, and liberation. While he was already leading us to take possession of our respective Promised Lands, he kept drawing us closer to his heart in preparation. While I was serving Catherine's vision God made me ready for mine. And weeks before the time was ripe for Catherine to enter hers, God send me off to get closer to my Promised Land.

But the most amazing thing in this whole process was, that God answered our prayers not just on the level we asked for, oh no. While we were mainly focussing on cleaning up Catherine's little business, he saw the big picture. He didn't just change one house, we started noticing a shift in the whole commercial sector. Rival businesses started to look to Catherine for guidance regarding the future of their trade. They started changing things up in their own businesses without really knowing why. The blessing God was pouring onto Catherine and her family was flowing through her towards the whole commercial sector. That is what it means to live in the Promised Land.

In 2007, during my lifechanging trip to Israel, Hanna, our guide in Jerusalem, brought us to the Zion Gate. She pointed to the bullet holes all around the gate, remnants of Israel's fight for the old city, and she said: "I want you to take a look at those bullet holes. That is what it looks like when a nation fights for their inheritance and destiny." I couldn't help asking myself whether I had my own Zion Gates, whether I had ever fought to get what God had promised to give me. At that point I couldn't think of any. But in me awoke the desire to hold on to what God had promised me. To remind him and myself, what he had spoken into my heart. And to prepare myself to fight for what he had for me. It can cost us to reach and inhabit our Promised Land. It can take a long time of holding on, constantly reminding yourself and God of the things he said and promised, and praying for breakthroughs. But it is worth it, it is your inheritance and destiny.

Maybe you don't know what your vision is. Maybe you have been wandering around in the desert for so long, you lost sight of it. Maybe you struggle to believe whether this Promised Land could be real at all. Maybe you never felt like a fish in water. Then turn towards the one who wants to promise you a life in his hands, his abundance, and his grace. Ask him what he has for you. Let him restore your old dreams and give you new ones. Let him show you what a life in his hands could be like. Let him draw you to himself and show you his love and grace. So that he may set you as an example for the relationship Man was made for and let his light shine through you.

"Heavenly Father, I long to live a life in your hands. I long to be yours, to live in the rhythm of your heartbeat, and like a fish in water. Please be my source of all security, provision, and fulfilment and set me as an example for the world to see the relationship Man was made for. Let your love shine through me. And while I am still in the desert, change my slave's mindset, draw me ever closer to your heart and replace my lies with your truth: you are the only source of perfect security, unfailing provision, and everlasting fulfilment. My value is found in you alone. I will set my heart on you alone."

Your Promised Land is waiting for you. You are made to live there, made for this life in God's hands. Grasp him as the giver of value, security, provision, and fulfilment, and let him lead you into the land of his rest.

If he had built the Holy Temple for us

The fifth thing God institutes to establish a place of encounter is to create a dwelling among his people. He tells Moses to build the Tabernacle, the Tent of Meeting. As a point of reference, he shows him the heavenly Tent of Meeting in a vision and has Israel build one just like it, following exact specifications. It's the place for offerings, the place to receive judgement, the place to encounter God's presence, the place to ask forgiveness, the place to receive mercy and restoration, the place to get guidance. While other deities had temples to offer up sacrifices as appeasement and mitigation, this is a place of communion. And, again, it sets Israel apart from all other nations in the world: they are God's people, he dwells among them.

In the 40 years in the desert, the Tabernacle always builds the centre of Israel's camp, with the people settling around it, turned towards it. God's constant presence is the centre of their lives. It is always the first thing they pack up whenever Israel sets out to a new location along their journey, the very first thing to be transported and to be set up in their new camp. Behind the carts which transport the parts of the tent follow the priests with the Ark of the Covenant, and only then the rest of the people with all their possessions. So no matter where they set up camp next, the first thing to arrive is God's dwelling place. His cloud leads them and where it stops the tent is set up. So whenever the people reach a new location, the Tent of Meeting, of encounter, and communion, is already set up and they settle around it.

How amazing is it, that the Holy God, the Almighty, the Sovereign Lord wants to live among his people? He is so different from all other gods. He is the I AM, the eternal one, he exists, is alive, is tangible, and longs for relationship. So much so that he is willing to confine himself to a fixed location, making himself constantly available to them. For the first time since the fall of Man God allows humans to come this close, to live so near his presence. Not because they deserve it, but because he longs for them to be his.

The Tabernacle, built in the image of the heavenly Tent of Meeting, stands in a courtyard where the Altar for Burnt Offering and the Basin for Washing stand before the tent. The tent itself is separated into two areas by a heavy curtain. The front two thirds build the Holy Place, where the Table of the Showbread, the golden Lampstand, and the Altar of Incense are housed. The hindmost third is partitioned off as the Holy of Holies, where the Ark of the Covenant is. So the courtyard is devoted to atonement and purification, attracting God's forgiveness and grace. The Holy Place is devoted to worship and thankfulness, attracting God's provision and help. And the Holy of Holies is devoted to encountering God at the core of his covenant and receiving his fulfilment.

This setup, again, mirrors God's journey and process with us. When he draws us to himself, we first experience his salvation and perfect security through Jesus' sacrifice and the power of his blood. Then he reveals himself, his love, and his grace to us and we experience his unfailing provision. All so he can then have communion with us at the core of his covenant and we can experience his everlasting fulfilment. Because Jesus came to fulfil God's covenant by becoming the eternal Passover lamb, our eternal Priest, and the eternal Temple to encounter the Heavenly Father, we can experience God's constant presence in our lives every day. Whenever I make God the centre of any decision and process, and seek him as the provider of all good things, I will attract his closeness and blessing in my life.

So, the Holy God, the Almighty, the Sovereign Lord still very much wants to live among us! He still is the I AM, the eternal one, he is still alive and tangible, and still longs for relationship. So much so that he gave his only begotten son to offer us salvation through Jesus' sacrifice, provision of all good things through Jesus as our intermediary before the Lord, and fulfilment through Jesus becoming our eternal Temple and the way to the Father. Not because we deserve it, but because he longs for us to be his. And neither our fallen nature, nor our brokenness, nor our disobedience keep him from reaching for us and making a way so that we may come back to the place where we belong: back into his arms, back into his presence, back into his heart. He makes himself available to us, holding nothing back, and brings us true fulfilment through a life in his hands.

All I have to do to see his presence and blessing in my life is to have him dwell at the centre of it, and turn toward him with any decision and process I go through at the moment. To let go and put my life into his hands. To put my heart, my fears, my hopes, my rights, and my tears on God's altar and give myself as a living sacrifice to attract his Holy Fire. Whenever I do, I start to see his hand in my life. He shows me ways I didn't see on my own. He gives me answers I needed. He comforts me, exchanges my fear for his love. He heals me, and gives me strength and guidance for the next step. What I hoped for and what I thought I deserved he exchanges for what I actually need and what will draw me closer to him. The more of my life

I give up, the more I gain of his. And the more everything makes sense.

In an episode of the TV-show Friends one character meets a person who doesn't own a television set, and reacts to this with: "What's all your furniture pointed at?" That is the line that pops into my head whenever I talk to someone who doesn't really understand my life in God's hands. It low-key startles me every time, because I can't imagine it differently anymore. My life makes just so much more sense when it is pointed at God in the centre. And the more I put on the altar, the easier it gets. I have seen him work everything for my good so many times now, I simply can't ignore it anymore. Whenever I let go of old habits, old defences, and old sources of provision, and instead turn to God, he faithfully plucks me off the cliff I cling to and plants me by the waters. So that I may send out my roots to the stream, straighten up, and grow strong in him.

God led me through my desert by having me lose my best friends. When I finally surrendered and put him in the centre of this process, everything changed. Sacrificing my heart, my pain, my sense of justice, my longing for retribution, and my hope for justification on his altar, attracted his holy fire and blessing. His comfort for my tears, his healing for my wounds, his protection for my heart. That is the blessing of the altar I sacrificed my heart on. And on top of that God gave me authority to help others let go of the cliffs they are clinging to and trust God to plant them by the waters.

When you look at the Old Testament, building an altar for God was a common occurrence and reaction whenever someone had an encounter with him. It is also very common for God's presence to last in these places of sacrifice. After the Lord showed the Promised Land to Abraham for the first time and with it the blessing he planned to bestow onto his descendants, Abraham built an altar, sacrificed, and worshipped. The blessing must have lasted in that place for at least two generations, because very near there Jacob encountered God as well, appearing to him in a dream of a ladder leading to heaven.

When David had just been crowned king of Israel, he wanted to bring the Ark of the Covenant from Shiloh to Jerusalem. Unfortunately, he didn't hold to God's commands regarding its transport, and had to see someone perish after touching it. But the family whose land he left the Ark at experienced a significant blessing of fruitfulness. So much so that David dared to try again and eventually succeeded in moving the Ark into his city. To this day, the stones in Shiloh are blessed with God's presence. At least, that is what it feels like to me whenever I am there. God's presence changes things. And it is always stronger wherever someone has given a sacrifice of faith in one way or another.

I have a huge wingback chair in my living room. It is my second favourite place to talk to God, after the outdoors. When it's cold outside or the weather is bad, I curl up in my chair, feeling like a little girl on her father's lap, and turn to God. Because of this ritual of seeking him sitting in my chair, it's also the place I easily find him. Because I give my day, my heart, my everything to him sitting in that chair, I attract his presence there. And because I ask him to speak to me sitting in my chair, I easily hear his voice there. Sometimes when I have a friend over and we chat about what God says and does in our lives, I find myself pointing to the chair to emphasise whatever I am sharing about God. Simply because in my mind my revelations of God's goodness are somehow tied to the place I received them. That is the blessing of the altar I built in my chair by giving myself to God there.

Apart from the altars I build, maintain, and serve at in my life by offering God my heart, efforts, time, and strength, my life is also blessed by altars others around me built and maintain. Since I can remember my Mom says: "God with you" whenever she sees us off, consciously putting us into his hands. This has given me and my siblings the assurance: we don't need to be afraid, no matter where we are, because the Almighty is with us, protecting us, guiding us. So what on this earth could be frightening?

My friend Lydia has built and maintains a very special altar in her life by waiting for the Holy Spirit. It is natural to her to sometimes spend hours inviting him, seeking his presence, and then diving into it, embracing whatever he wants to do or say. Whenever he reveals something to her, she asks him for more details, listening to his stories unfolding in her heart, delving ever deeper into God's love. Seeking him together with her in prayer is amazingly easy and always goes incredibly deep, because the altar in her life has a direct, constantly open line into God's presence. Its blessing is making it easy to encounter God on a deep level.

Remember Catherine from the last chapter? Her story with God actually didn't begin with her conversion. It started a few years before. She and her family had decided to expand and refocus their business and started construction for that new expansion. Since construction is a messy and time-consuming ordeal, sales figures dropped and the banks began to put pressure on them. So, as a last resort, Catherine one evening decided to put the whole business into God's hands in prayer. Even though she didn't know him, whether he even existed, or how to pray, she took her kids, barely teenagers at the time, and the director of her company, had them stand in a circle in the middle of the construction site and prayed: "Dear God, we are at the end of our rope. Please, build this company, this new department, and this new house." Without even really knowing what she was saying she offered her business to God, who accepted her sacrifice, brought his Holy Fire down on it, and did just what Catherine had asked him to do: he built the company after his heart. Now, his presence and his blessing undeniably dwell there. Working there has truly blessed me in ways I could never have imagined.

The ministry and community I live in and work at maintain an altar built over 50 years ago. The founders, after experiencing the Lord in a new way, longed for unity in the body of Christ. They saw the differences between the denominations as enriching and wanted to establish a place where anyone could experience God without restriction. So they lived together, everyone bringing their gifts, talents, and most of all their unique way to live the relationship with the God they loved, building a tapestry of faith. It cost them a lot of struggles, tears, devotion, empathy, and self-abandonment. But it brought them the Holy Fire of God, his presence, and his blessing. Which, to this day, build the foundation for a place where God can move without restriction and people from any denomination can encounter him.

Maybe you've never made God the centre of your life. Maybe you still dislike the concept of offering anything to him. Maybe you have never dared to put yourself into his hands. Maybe you can't imagine letting go of that cliff you've been clinging to for so long. Maybe you fear what might happen if you did. Maybe letting go still feels too much like a sacrifice not worth the price. Maybe you fear what God might want to have from you or might want to make you do with your life, if he only gets his hands on you. Or maybe, like me, you see how God has asked you several times already to let go and give your heart to him, but you never went through with it.

Then let me tell you this: God wants you to be his and wants to dwell right in the centre of your life. He held nothing back to create a way for you to meet him and know him. He is your perfect saviour, your unfailing provider, and your everlasting fulfilment. When his fire comes down upon the offering on the altar and burns away all the fat, it turns the offering into the best version, into the healthiest meat to eat. What you sacrifice he won't rip anything away from you, but will transform it into the best version. He will not claim renunciation from you, will not reduce you to a humbled slave, will not oppress you, and will not leave you wanting. Don't believe the lie that he asks too much of you. Don't believe the lie that he only wants to have you serve him. Don't believe the lie that he wants to keep good stuff from you. Know that nothing he takes from you is worth having. Know that when he plucks you off that cliff he will plant you by the water and you will grow into something you never knew you could be. Know that whatever you give him he will turn into something greater, easier, deeper. It will attract his Holy fire, his blessing, and his presence. Test him on it, if you don't believe me. Ask him to take just that one little thing you can bring yourself to let go of and ask him to transform it. So that the next time it will be so much easier for you to trust him and let go. All you have to do is ask.

"Heavenly Father, I want to know you as you are. I want to see your presence change my life. Part of me still doesn't know whether trusting you is such a good idea. But I heard of your goodness, your grace, and your love, and I long to see your hand in my life. So today I let go, today I invite you to accept my offering and turn it into whatever you have for me. Today I want to build the first little altar to attract your presence and your blessing. Holy Spirit, please teach me to make God the centre of my life and open my eyes to his goodness."

Letting go and have God transform whatever I give him has become a pleasure in my life. Witnessing God's goodness in action when he plants me by the water and lets me grow strong is a grace beyond measure. Undeserved, certainly not earned this grace may be. But, oh, it is such a beautiful life, this life in his presence and under his blessing.

God's perfect fulfilment

The last five verses of the Dayenu, the "Five Stanzas of Closeness with God" perfectly show what God does to prepare a place in his fulfilling presence and a life in his hands for us. The five things he instituted among his people establish his heavenly dimension in a fallen world. So that we may see and learn what the life and relationship Man was made for should be like. They show us the place we truly belong, the place we will find true fulfilment, the place we are truly at home, the place where we were truly made to be.

A weekly destined and consecrated day to let go, rest, be restored, and enjoy each other. An eternal covenant, a commitment of unrepayable love, unflinching and unyielding. Guidelines to his blessing, to a life in peace, justice, health, and prosperity. A life in the Promised Land, where things come easy, without great struggle, like a fish in water. A dwelling place for God in the centre of life, a place of deep encounter and transforming presence.

These verses reveal God's heart for relationship like nothing else in the Bible. He made us for himself, to love us, and to love creation with us. He wants to be with us and he knows: we need to be with him. It's what made him plant the Tree of Knowledge in the Garden of Eden. Made him create Israel out of a barren family to set as an example for the world. Made him establish a place where he revealed himself, and made him give his son to prepare an eternal way back to him. He is love. He couldn't keep himself from doing all this. Because he can't not love us. It's who he is, who he was, and who he will be eternally. He made us out of his love because he loves us. All the steps to break us free, all the miracles to provide for us, he took just to draw us back to him. Because he longs for us he is still asking: Will you be mine?

Establishing a relationship with God is not about making room for him in our lives. It is not about trying to remember to involve him sometimes. It is not about hoping he would somehow bless whatever we decided our lives to be. It is about starting a new life by stepping into his dimension, where his rules instead of the rules of the world apply. Where he forgives and loves a sinner who repents. Where forgiving brings freedom and letting go of revenge brings healing. Where two fish and five loaves of bread feed 5000. Where tithing brings financial abundance. Where serving others brings respect and authority. Where God blesses those who trust him. Where he will let all things work for the good of those who love him. Where he is the source of perfect salvation, unfailing provision, and eternal fulfilment.

The Heavenly Father has done everything needed to bring us back to him. All we need to do is ask ourselves what our answer to all this is. Where are we in that process? What part of our relationship with God is already established and where should we invest our hearts and lives to grow closer to him? Let the Holy Spirit draw you into a deeper encounter with God. Let him show you which area of your life he wants to transform in his presence. Let him take your offering and bring down his Holy Fire and his blessing. The next step on our way into his heart is always the closest to him we ever gotten and the best one we ever took.

In one aspect the last five verses of the Dayenu differ from the ten before. On top of being a revelation of God's love and heart for closeness they are also a guideline to a healthy relationship. The five things God instituted as a platform for a deeper relationship with him also work perfectly as a solid foundation for a deep friendship or fulfilling marriage. We need time specifically dedicated to one another to build a relationship. We need commitment, the decision to stick together. We need rules of conduct as guidelines to blessing, written on our hearts. We need a life together, where we complement each other and are a blessing for the other person, as much as they are a blessing to us. We need places and times of deep encounter, where the other person is the sole focus for us. And just like in our relationship with God it is good to be free from our past, our slavery, our false idols, and our slave-drivers to enjoy a loving relationship. Then, we can see and know the other person as a provider of good things and as a blessing. Then, our relationship can be a union of two people that is greater than the sum of all parts.

This is how far God's salvation goes. He doesn't just save us, bless us, and fulfil us. He breaks us free and showers us with grace so we can enjoy not only him but each other on a deeper, more meaningful level. And see his freedom not only in heaven but already here on earth in every single aspect of our lives.

Dayenu fulfilled

Truly enough

When the Holy Spirit revealed the essence of this book to me on that Seder evening all those years ago, he did it by repeating every sentence my father read in different words. Words that spoke of my life rather than telling Israel's story. With every verse he said, he drove this truth ever deeper into my mind, my heart, and my soul. His words were concise and extensive at the same time.

If he had found me in my oppression and hadn't shown me how much I need him, it would have been enough.

If he had shown me how much I need him and hadn't freed me from false security, the substitutes for his provision, and false hopes, it would have been enough.

If he had freed me from false security, the substitutes for his provision, and false hopes and hadn't saved me from the eternal death I deserved for my sins, it would have been enough.

If he had saved me from the eternal death I deserved for my sins and hadn't given me authority over my past and turned what was supposed to destroy me into a way of freeing others, it would have been enough.

If he had given me authority over my past and turned what was supposed to destroy me into a way of freeing others and hadn't opened ways for me where there was no way out, it would have been enough.

If he had opened ways for me where there was no way out and hadn't made the way he opened for me easy to walk on, it would have been enough.

If he had made the way he opened for me easy to walk on and hadn't made me untouchable for my past oppression, it would have been enough.

If he had made me untouchable for my past oppression and hadn't provided for all my needs, it would have been enough.

If he had provided for all my needs and hadn't taken care of my basic supplies in my hardest times, it would have been enough.

If he had taken care of my basic supplies in my hardest times and hadn't given me a weekly day of letting go, resting, restoration, and relationship, it would have been enough.

If he had given me a weekly day of letting go, resting, restoration, and relationship and hadn't offered me his covenant and called me his, it would have been enough.

If he had offered me his covenant and called me his and hadn't given me guidelines to his blessing and rules for a good life, it would have been enough.

If he had given me guidelines to his blessing and rules for a good life and hadn't given me a life in his hands, with his provision, peace, and freedom, it would have been enough.

If he had given me a life in his hands, with his provision, peace, and freedom and hadn't given me a place to encounter him and receive his salvation, provision, and fulfilment, it would have been enough.

Because he gave it all, perfect salvation, unfailing provision, and everlasting fulfilment, it now is truly enough.

I could immediately see God's hand in my life; his way of breaking me free, guiding me, and providing for me was so obvious all of a sudden. I could see how every one of the fifteen steps out of slavery into a life in his hands, his freedom, and his fulfilment, is still a miracle on its own. And it was immediately obvious to me that he was showing me both a way to adapt the story of Israel's Exodus to my life and a timeline to use as a reference to see where I stand right now and were God wants to lead me. No wonder he wants Israel to remember this every year on Passover and every week on Shabbat, as if they had lived through it themselves.

When I looked at the Seder table that night, laden with numerous special foods designed to remind his people of the life they left behind, the salvation they experienced, and the blessings God showed them ever since, I felt a slight pang of jealousy. I wished I could have such a wonderful visual representation of the great things God did in my life. I wished for an evening of joy where my family and I focus on rejoicing in the Lord for his great deeds. But with the jealousy also came an immense joy. About the way he sets me free to love him and others the way he made me to love. About the perfection of his salvation, his provision, and his fulfilment. About his beautiful heart and love for us that he showed me that night. And about the much deeper meaning of the comparatively simple act of communion I could grasp now.

I always loved celebrating communion, but how much more now that I can see what I am celebrating here. Yes, it would be enough to rejoice in Jesus' sacrificial death and his resurrection. It is, after all, the greatest miracle and show of God's love for us. But truly grasping the journey of salvation, provision, and fulfilment that is completed in Jesus becoming my eternal Passover lamb, my eternal Priest, and my eternal Temple to encounter my Heavenly Father, deeply changed me. Now I can celebrate all fifteen steps, rather than just the most important one. And even though we say just one of the steps is enough to praise God forever, just one wouldn't really be enough, would it? No, because God's freedom is only complete after all fifteen steps; we only truly know him as he is after all fifteen revelations.

I read a blog once, where the writer, a practicing Jew, talked about the Dayenu song and the Seder evenings of his childhood. He and his siblings oftentimes burst out laughing when singing it, because it just felt so much like saying 'Enough already'. Which was exactly what they felt like shouting after an hour of traditional prayers, Bible readings, and religious practices, especially because they were hungry by then and still not allowed to eat. I can empathize. A Seder evening can go on for a long time. To a child, having to listen to the story of the Exodus on an empty stomach can feel almost as long as it actually took Israel to get from Egypt to the Promised Land. Of course you want to shout 'Enough already!'

But even though every single step is a miracle and reason to praise God for all eternity, none of them would be truly enough on its own. What an immeasurable grace it is that it's God himself who decides when it is enough! As I was talking about this with God one day I asked him: "I am so glad you didn't just find me but led me all fifteen steps into your perfect freedom. I am so thankful it is up to you to say 'Enough already', and no one else. But when did you?"

He answered with an exceptionally clear vision of Jesus on the cross, saying with his last breath: "Now it is enough!" There on the cross it was finally truly enough. With Jesus becoming our eternal Passover lamb, our eternal Priest, and our eternal Temple to encounter the Heavenly Father our salvation was fulfilled. Nothing in the world can or need to be added to this. The Cross is enough because it brings to a close what God already planned with the planting of Eden and started with Abraham.

When he had received the drink, Jesus said, "It is finished." With that, he bowed his head and gave up his spirit. (John 19:30)

With the Cross, the story of Israel's and of our salvation is finished. The End. We now have the chance to live happily ever after.

Perfect fulfilment through perfect peace

This clear vision of Jesus and his last words made me wonder whether he maybe actually said 'Dayenu' that day. So I asked my Dad about it and he checked his Hebrew bible. He didn't, he said something else and I can't remember the Hebrew phrase anymore. But I clearly remember my Dad saying: "The word he said has the same root as Shalom. So he said it is pacified, it is fulfilled, Shalom is made." This has stuck with me. Because Shalom means so much more than peace, as in the absence of war. It means inner peace, completion, fulfilment. It means being the person I am made to be, in the place where I am made to be, at the time I am made to be, doing the things I am made to do.

That is perfect fulfilment. Being the person I am made to be: God's child and friend, perfectly free from pain, sickness, and suffering. Being where I am made to be: Under his mercy and grace, rooted at the water of his perfect provision where I can grow strong. Being when I am made to be: In his calling, living in the rhythm of his heartbeat. Doing the things I am made to do: What comes easy and naturally to me, because God has tailor-made me for this with the right gifts, talents, and motivation. Fulfilling my destiny as a blessing from God for everyone I encounter. That is what Shalom means.

The great Christian author and apologist C.S. Lewis once described the process of being delivered and transformed by God like this:

> *Imagine yourself as a living house. God comes in to rebuild that house. At first, perhaps, you can understand what He is doing. He is getting the drains right and stopping the leaks in the roof and so*

> *on; you knew that those jobs needed doing and so you are not surprised. But presently He starts knocking the house about in a way that hurts abominably and does not seem to make any sense. What on earth is He up to? The explanation is that He is building quite a different house from the one you thought of - throwing out a new wing here, putting on an extra floor there, running up towers, making courtyards. You thought you were being made into a decent little cottage: but He is building a palace. He intends to come and live in it Himself. (C.S. Lewis, Mere Christianity)*

When I first read this passage many years ago, it brought me enormous comfort. At the time I was struggling with condemnation because I felt stuck on a rollercoaster of having deep, life-changing encounters with God, only to feel like I had fallen out of his presence somehow shortly after. It did hurt abominably and it didn't make sense. It was like walking with God and then running into a wall at full speed. What was I doing wrong? Why did I keep running into walls? Shame and condemnation about my obvious inability to stay in God's presence started to crush me. Until I read that passage in Mere Christianity and the Holy Spirit said: "The Father is guiding you closer to his heart, up a staircase. He is walking backwards, so you can see his face upon you, and he beckons you to follow him. Whenever you feel like you somehow lost his presence, it is just because he went up a step and wants you to follow him to this new level, where you will find him again."

What a relief this revelation was. God wasn't constantly fighting against my leaks and decay, he was building a palace! So he, the King, may come and live in it! So I really love the Lewis quote. But, and I hope Mr. Lewis will forgive me, I think the image is a little off. Instead of being a cottage God is turning into a palace by throwing out new wings, putting on extra floors, running up towers, and making courtyards, I find myself to be a palace who thinks themselves to just be a cottage in need of renovation. So when God starts the big work of opening up the wings, turrets, and halls that have been in disuse and decay for so long that I didn't even know they existed, it comes as a shocking surprise. But it isn't God forcefully turning me into something I am not but rather my image of myself needing to be expanded to fit everything I truly am. Becoming the true palace I was made to be, with every wing reopened, and every courtyard freed from brambles, is what Shalom truly means. And it is what God invites us to when he finds us in our oppression. A life in his Shalom, in his perfect fulfilment.

In Israel you can often see the line "Pray for the peace of Jerusalem" in various artistic versions, from postcards to chiseled into stone. I love that, now that I know Shalom means to live one's destiny to the fullest. Because Jerusalem's destiny is to be the place where God dwells and reveals himself. To be the place where God's blessing starts and then flows into the world, bringing Shalom, God's perfect fulfilment to every nation. So If I pray for the Shalom of Jerusalem, I pray for the whole world to be flooded with God's blessing and grace. If I pray for Jerusalem to fulfil her destiny, I pray for the whole world and myself to be transformed by God's lifechanging presence.

So where am I?

Ever since the Holy Spirit revealed to me God's process to freedom exemplified in the story of the Exodus, the Dayenu is my go-to reference whenever I want to know where I stand at the moment. If I feel like I have my back up against the wall, I now ask the Holy Spirit: "Is this because you need to show me the true state of affairs right now? Or do you want to unmask one of my false idols? Do I need you to make a way before me or shall I trust you to provide my basic supplies? Do I need to see you save me and provide for me or do you want to drown my oppressors behind me?"

No matter what it is I am struggling with, to ask God to keep doing his thing and following him is the best thing ever. Because in every situation I will get to know him better and will trust him more afterwards. And I will step into greater freedom and deeper fulfilment. Even the most unbearable circumstances offer me the chance to encounter God as I have never seen him before.

It requires training, a little ritual of reflection, to develop the habit of involving God in your life like this. Maybe you are not used to having conversations with the Holy Spirit at all. Maybe you feel like there is a certain amount of spiritual maturity needed to actually hear God answer when you ask him something. I certainly thought so growing up. I was about twenty when I first started to ask God to teach me to recognize his voice. I knew Jesus said that his sheep listen to his voice and follow him (John 10:27). And I thought, well, if I want to follow Jesus, I need to know the sound of his voice. So I kept asking him to speak to me, about literally anything. And he did. At first, every word he said was accompanied by a little jolt of adrenaline, so I could clearly distinguish him talking from my own thoughts. I learned, his voice always sounds loving and important. And it always stands out from my thoughts as something I hadn't thought before, so it often makes me stop in my tracks.

To teach me to trust my judgement on this, God started to give me things I had to say in front of the congregation during Sunday service. And he made sure, people would come to me afterwards and tell me how God spoke to them through me. When I was used to hearing him speak, God stopped the jolts of adrenaline, I don't need them anymore, I recognize his voice immediately now. Only once did he use that jolt since, in a situation where he wanted me to do something he knew would be highly uncomfortable for me, because I had to overstep certain boundaries to obey him. So he wanted to make extra sure I knew it was him telling me to do it.

I underwent this whole training to learn to hear God's voice. But I have also seen God starting to talk to people right away, sometimes without them even giving their lives to Jesus beforehand. My favourite story about this happened while I was in the pool at the hotel I worked at. It was part of my job to take the guests' kids swimming for an hour every day, play with them, and let them have a fun holiday. It had just become public that I would leave said hotel soon and two girls wanted to hear the whole story about why and where I was going. Since I was working there because God had told me to do so, and I was also leaving because he was sending me somewhere else, they heard a lot about God in my story. After I had finished, the younger of the two girls was curious to hear me pray. So I offered to pray for her. Her sister wanted in on that action, so I started to pray for both of them.

Whenever I pray for someone who doesn't know God that well, I always explain to them: "When I pray for someone, I always just say whatever comes to me. If I say something that makes you think 'I would really like that to happen' you can just say yes to it in your heart. If I don't say anything for you, you can just shrug it off." So I prayed, and afterwards the girls looked happy, but they also had questions. "I can't imagine God really existing", said the younger one, "he is supposed to have created the whole world, but how would that have worked?"

"Well", I answered, "in the Bible it says that God spoke and called the world into existence. I can totally believe that, because I have seen him do that in my life many times. When I am stuck and ask him to speak into that situation, things start to come into existence. You can just ask him to speak, and he will." By then, our swimming hour was over and I had to clean the pool area with a squeegee. While I was working, the elder of the girls stayed in the pool, diving under and coming back up a couple of times. When she emerged from the water for the third time, she said: "It really works. I asked him to speak and he did." And under water she went again. When she got back up, she asked me: "What does God's voice sound like to you?" "Well, a bit like my own thoughts, yet different. Whatever he says always sounds important and immediately makes me stop and think about it for a moment." She beamed and nodded. "I think, he sounds so loving!" she then said. To which I could only reply with: "Yes! He always sounds loving! Even when he has to scold me, he still sounds loving!" and give her a high five. It was just so incredibly cool that God chose to speak to this young girl, just because she asked him to, right in the middle of the pool.

He is still the I AM. He still, with every fibre of his being, invites us to get to know him. Still invites us to come back into the relationship we were made for and into the perfect freedom he has for us. Being free from everything and dependent only on him. And no matter where we are in our lives, we are definitely somewhere on that timeline between completely oppressed and totally free in him. So all we have to do to keep moving forward, is to ask him to take us the next step, allow him to reveal himself to us as we have never known him before. If he can and wants to speak to a girl in a pool, he will answer you.

"God, I feel like I have my back up against the wall and I don't really know why. Please show me where I am in your timeline to your perfect freedom and take me the next step. I long to know you as you are, please take the slave out of me to take me out of slavery. Please reveal yourself to me as the source of all perfect security, unfailing provision, and everlasting fulfilment. Take me out of my oppression and into your Shalom, where I can be who you made me to be. Holy Spirit, please lead me into the truth."

As for me and my household

After several centuries of Egypt, a mighty show of God's power as the saviour, 40 years in the dessert cared for by God the provider, and years of taking possession of the Promised Land led by the God who fights for them, Israel has truly settled in the land of his Shalom. They are where they are supposed to be, living in peace and abundance. Joshua, Moses' successor as leader of the people, has gotten old and is about to die. As his last official act he calls the elders, leaders, judges, and officials of every tribe together at Shechem to give them an exhorting farewell speech. Just like the Dayenu does at every Seder evening, he recounts all the great deeds God did to lead Israel out of slavery into the Promised Land. "You know with all your heart and soul that not one of the promises the Lord your God gave you has failed. Every promise has been fulfilled. You have seen what the Lord your God has done to all the nations around you. It was the Lord your God who fought for you. So obey his laws, follow his guidelines to his blessing. Do not associate with the nations that remain among you. Do not call upon their gods, but hold on fast to I AM, your God. Be careful to love him. If you let go of him, he will let go of you, and you will perish from the land he has given to you." (See Joshua 24:1-13)

And then Joshua presents them with a choice:

"Now fear the Lord and serve him with all faithfulness. Throw away the gods your ancestors worshipped beyond the Euphrates River and in Egypt, and serve the Lord. But if serving the Lord seems undesirable to you, then choose for yourselves this day whom you will serve, whether the gods your ancestors served beyond the Euphrates, or the gods of the Amorites, in whose land you are

living. But as for me and my household, we will serve the Lord."
(Joshua 24:14-15)

After everything, we still have a choice. Every day of our lives God allows us to choose between self-determination and the freedom found in him. Even after everything he did to lead us out of oppression into his Shalom, he still and forever puts our will above his own. Because he loves us and wants us to be free to love him in return. It is completely up to us. Do we say yes to his offer of salvation, provision, and fulfilment in his hands today? Or do we hold on to our old sources of protection, life, and hope? Do we dare to follow his invitation to come closer and experience him? Or do we rather trust the familiar, oppressive as it may be? It is entirely our decision.

All I can say is: this decision becomes easier and easier the more I answer with yes. Because every yes I gave God as an answer has brought me much closer to his heart and into his perfect freedom, his perfect Shalom. With every revelation of an aspect of his character and love it becomes more and more my heart's desire to live a life in his hands. Nothing I let go of and sacrificed on his altar was actually worth keeping. Everything he took away from me was good riddance. Whatever I laid in his hands has become so much better, bigger, more Spirit-filled. Whenever I ask him to speak, he doesn't speak mere words, he speaks life and calls things into existence. I know with all my heart and soul that not one of the promises God gave me has failed. Every promise has been fulfilled. The more I let him save me the more I realize: living in dependence on him is true freedom. The freedom I was made for.

So I want to present you with the same choice: to follow God the I AM, who made you to be free from any oppression and suffering to live in a loving relationship with him, or to follow the familiar substitutes for his fullness. He will not be appalled by your pick. He knows what is holding you back. And he will never force you to let go of your craggy cliff. He will never rip you from the only security you've known so far. So it's absolutely okay if your answer to his love is still no today. Just know this: he will keep reaching for you, sending you signs of his love, showing himself to you in nature, people, and your own heart. Because just as much as Jesus couldn't bear to see his Father's heart broken and incomplete, the Father cannot bear to see you broken and incomplete without him. So he will look for any possible way to call to your heart and reveal himself as your true salvation, provision, and fulfilment. If your answer is no, I wish you the tiny bit of courage needed to look for the signs of God's love for you. So you will maybe one day dare to give the tiny yes needed for the first step into his freedom. It will be the greatest step in your life so far.

Dayenu applied – an epilogue

Each verse of the Dayenu is an incredible stand-alone event, each exemplifying one of 15 individual revelations God uses to make himself known to us. They are each distinct and each invite us a distinct step closer to God. But just like it was a continuous journey for Israel with every step building on the previous one, it can also be a continuous process to follow for us. A road we can choose to take, whenever we find ourselves oppressed in some way. Following this road, this process to receive God's perfect freedom, has become an extraordinary tool of self-care for the soul to me. No matter if I find myself in sin, bound by my past, or oppressed by the enemy in some way, I always use the Dayenu as a guide to seek God and let him set me free. It is an extremely versatile and extremely effective tool to work through stuff with God. So to end this book I want to give you an example of how I apply the Dayenu in everyday life and how I use it as a guide to prayer, counselling, and self-care for my soul.

In the chapter about the Shabbat I already mentioned my burn-out. The road I took to get back to mental and physical health was very much modelled after the journey God took his people out of slavery and into the promised land.

As I mentioned before my seven weeks of fatigue started with a common cold, so I was seeing a doctor regularly, mainly for the sick certificate but also because I naturally wanted to know what was wrong with me. Why was I feeling so weak? For five weeks the doctor kept saying it was perfectly normal for a virus to take this long to leave the body. So for five weeks I was not even entertaining the thought the reason for my fatigue might be psychological, even though a friend had already suggested that possibility in week three. Just like Israel I didn't see my oppression as the truly unbearable situation it was.

That changed quite abruptly when at the end of week five when, after a complete blood count and two electrocardiograms, the doctor simply said: "Well, there is no physical reason for you to feel the way you feel. It can only be one of two things. Either it is gynaecological or psychological. Do you suffer stress at work?" When I truthfully denied he didn't seem to believe me, because he continued: "Well, I will prescribe you a pharmaceutical which will give you the strength for everyday tasks." When he explained more, two things raised red flags in me: the side effects made it sound very much like an antidepressant and the words he used seemed very much chosen to avoid the word antidepressant. I felt manipulated and misunderstood, which overwhelmed me. With one little prescription my situation became immediately unbearable.

I needed this little shock. God had found me in my personal Egypt and made me realize my oppression. After talking the whole situation through with my brother and a counsellor friend I understood that my fatigue came from the stress of the years before rather than my life at the moment. Now that this was clear to me I addressed this problem head-on. I immediately knew, I was in verse one of the Dayenu. At least four more to go into God's freedom, no time to waste.

The next couple of days I deliberately spend time in prayer, asking God to guide me into his freedom. To bring judgement upon my oppressors and to show me my unbearable state more fully the Holy Spirit had me write down in detail any mental wounds, injuries, emotional assaults, excessive demands, and attacks I had suffered in the 11 years of my previous job. It turned out to be quite a collection. Safe in God's arms I cried about each and every thing on that list, mourned it, debunked what needed to be debunked, and received God's comfort. It was an exhausting process, but oh so relieving!

After that we looked at the false gods I had hoped to receive security, provision, and fulfilment from. They were over-eagerness, a false sense of duty, and a desperate need to prove myself, and they brought fear of failure and pressure to perform along with them. No wonder I was fatigued. No wonder God had wanted me to slow down and let him take this awful burden from me. By telling me I had not disappointed him but had done exactly what he had wanted me to do in my former job, and by telling me his love for me alone defined my worth and purpose, he helped me let go of my false gods. I found myself in him again and could now receive his vision for my life once again.

Because of step 4, because God gave his firstborn to save me from the death I deserved, I could forgive the emotional injuries and attacks, could repent from serving my false gods, could receive freedom from my oppression, and healing for my wounds. Being allowed to cast all my burdens on him and receiving his forgiveness was both relieving and healing. What an incredible mercy!

And of course, after rescuing me so completely he showed me his grace by giving me the treasures of the land of my oppression: A much deeper understanding of the process of burn-out and the key to guide people through it. And what is more, a much deeper knowledge of my worth in him. It is his manifest eternal love that drives out all pressure to perform and fear of failure. And frees me completely so I can experience God as my provider and my fulfilment.

Casting my burdens on God, even the ones deep down that I hadn't realized I was carrying, was such a relief. And my body quickly picked up on that. My strength came back, not all at once but far faster than I had expected. Only two weeks after God took me the first step of the Dayenu I was able to go back to work. And after a week at work everything felt normal again. Because I had encountered God's perfect security, unfailing provision, and everlasting fulfilment, my situation was completely changed.

Maybe my case of burn-out doesn't sound half as severe as some of the situations you have experienced. Maybe the comparison with my few weeks of fatigue doesn't really work for you because you struggle with so much more right now. Then let me remind you: God is the same. If you were an entire nation, enslaved, broken, adjusted to an oppressed life, his deliverance would be truly enough to bring you into the land of his blessing. Your situation is not overwhelming to him. He knows the way out of your Egypt into his arms. And he can't wait to take you out of oppression and into his heart.

God's transforming love never fails to amaze me. No matter the place he finds us in, no matter the size or shape of our chains and shackles, his liberation will be perfect. And we will encounter him as our unfailing provider and our everlasting fulfilment. I hope and pray you will dare to trust him the next time you find yourself under some oppression or other. It is entirely up to you to say yes to him. His Yes stands and doesn't change. Just take the first step and be changed. It will be amazing.

Acknowledgements

God deserves my gratefulness and all my devotion. His perfect salvation, unfailing provision, and everlasting fulfilment again and again enriched my life. He is the true author of this book, because his story with his people alone made it possible. His love for us has me in awe every day.

Without my brother Tobias I would not have been able to have this book printed. His support kept me going. He challenged me when I wanted to hold back. His prayer and feedback kept me grounded and gave me direction.

Without my sister Kerstin and my best friend Stefanie this book would have had more mistakes and would have been a lot less easy to read. Their thoroughness is a valuable complement to me.

Without the encouragement of my sister Karen I would never have started writing in the first place. Because she took the aspirations of a twelve-year-old seriously, I started to develop my style.

Without the love, values, and the everyday faith of my parents I wouldn't be the woman I am today. My father's unshakeable consistency and my mother's liberating determination were and still are anchor and drive to me.